SWANGKEENOMIKS Rules the Roost!

(HOW all People can Prosper in a RIIT WAA, and Stop Polluting the Earth with Capitalist TRASH!)

By
The Worldwide People's Revolution!®

Book 039 ♥

(Page 3 shows a Photo of our Retirement Home before the Concrete Roof was Poured around more than 3 Miles of Steel Reinforcement Bars during just one Dreadful Day with a Concrete Pump Truck! It Required 2 Months of "Backbreaking" Work to get all of the Rebars in Place. There are 2 Layers of Rebars every 8-inches apart in both directions, being Wired Together, and Guaranteed to Endure for at least 40 Years, Thanks to Acid Rains from Capitalist Abominations. Otherwise, without those Acid Rains, it might Endure for a thousand Years, or more; but, only IF Swanky Cement were used to make the Correct Concrete! We intend to Cover the Roof with Ceramic Tiles to Protect it. P-5370. The Cover Photo shows a Trash Truck being Loaded for the Dump. P-1585.)

Copyright, Dedication and Introduction

By our Selected King's Chief Editor — Doctor Samuel Walker Edison, Ph.D., MA., BS and QC!

ISBN — 13: 978-1727-6473-27
ISBN — 10: 1727-6473-27

00-01 [_] This Inspired Book is COPYRIGHTED AD 2018—4020, by the Selected King of **The Worldwide People's Revolution!®**, who has been Dreaming about a NEW and Wonderful Economic System, which does not Rely on the Exploitation of Limited Natural Resources; but, rather, on the Exploitation of Abundant Natural Resources — such as some of those hundreds of thousands of Mountains of ROCKS and Oceans of Water, which will be Happy to Lend their "Services" to **"The New RIGHTEOUS One-World Government,"** which, with the Help of **"Seven Great Armies of Working Soldiers,"** will Transform those Mountains of Rocks into **"Beautiful Swanky PALACES!" (A New Concept in Living Habits — Swanky Palaces for Poor People!)**, Book 066. Yes, there are more than 5,000 Good Reasons and Great Advantages for Building and Living within the Borders of Beautiful Planned City States. {See www.Amazon.com for: **"The Right Design for Living!" (A List of Great Advantages for Building Beautiful Planned City States!) By The Worldwide People's Revolution!®** B-012.}

00-02 [_] All Rights are Reserved for the Sake of Humanity, most of whom are now Suffering in their Confused States of Extreme Poverty, who do not even have Fresh Clean Air to Breathe, Pure Living Water to Drink, nor Wholesome Natural Foods to Eat, much less Secure Self-air-conditioned Stone Dome Home Complexes to Live in, which are Fireproof, Hail-proof, Tornado-proof, Hurricane-proof, Flood-damage-proof, Rot-proof, Paint-proof, Termite-proof, Rat-proof, Mouse-proof, Snake-proof, Insurance-proof, and Tax-proof! Indeed, our Selected King Explains to us within this Inspired Book HOW all of that can be done for almost everyone in the Whole World, and without Borrowing any Money from any Gangster Banksters, nor going into Debt to anyone for anything. Therefore, Remember **"The Seven Basic Spiritual Building Blocks of LIFE!" (Faith, Hope, Trust, Love, Patience, Persistence and OBEDIENCE!)**, Book 036, which Building Blocks are also Necessary for Comprehending this Special Book, which contains Surprising and Enlightening Information, which most People have never Learned.

00-03 [_] No Portion of this Inspired Book shall be Reproduced by any Means for Sale without Written Permission from **The Worldwide People's Revolution!®** However, with that Permission, anyone in the World may Sell this Book for a Reasonable Profit, and KEEP 90 percent of the Net Profits: beCause our Selected King only wants 10% of the Net Profits for the Construction of **"The Great World TEMPLE of PEACE,"** which will be the Marvelous Headquarter for **"The New RIGHTEOUS One-World Government!" (HOW to Establish a Righteous One-World Government without Going to WAR!) By The Worldwide People's Revolution!®** Book 056. Yes, it will be the Tallest and Largest Building in the World, where all of the Elected Officials will Live and Work, without any Wasteful Campaigning for Election Deceptions: beCause each Potential Elected King or Queen will simply fill out and Post on the Internet **"The Complete SURVEYS of our VALUES!"** Book 059, for all Electors to Study, free of all Charges.

(HOW all People can Prosper in a RIIT WAA, and Stop Polluting the Earth with Capitalist TRASH!)

(HOW all People can Prosper in a RIIT WAA, and Stop Polluting the Earth with Capitalist TRASH!)

00-04 [_] Yes, that one Act of a World Congress will Save us Education Slaves, Work Slaves, Tax Slaves, Insurance Slaves, Interest Slaves, Rent Slaves, Transportation Slaves, Food Bills Slaves, Gas Bills Slaves, Water Bills Slaves, ElecTrickery Bills Slaves, Entertainment Bills Slaves, Telephone Bills Slaves, Childcare Slaves, and Endless Bills SLAVES of all Colors and Kinds TRILLIONS of Dollars, Worldwide, on Political Campaigns and Election Deceptions: beCause no such Campaigns are Needed for Determining WHO Qualifies to Rule Over us. Indeed, we must Learn what all such Candidates BELIEVE, before Electing them, which can best be done on the Internet, Free of Charge, which is a very Good Tool for Learning almost anything that a Person can Think of, including the Religious, Spiritual, Political, Governmental, Sexual, Social, Moral, Economic, Business, Labor, Habitual and Miscellaneous VALUES! Indeed, if you would like to Study the Values of our Selected King, you can find them in: **"Mark Twain Races for the PRESIDENCY!" (The 2020 Presidential Candidates Desperately Need Some STRONG Undefeatable COMPETITION!) By The Worldwide People's Revolution!® Book 033.**

00-05 [_] O Doctor Samuel Walker Edison, is the Selected King of **The Worldwide People's Revolution!®** another Worthless POLITICIAN?

00-06 [_] No Sir! He is an Inspired Author, Architect, Engineer, Stone Mason, Brick Layer, Tile Setter, Carpenter, Taylor, Printer, Book Binder, Inventor, Organic Gardener, Farmer, Plumber, Electrician, Chef, Cowboy, Butcher, Baker, Concrete Maker, Vietnam Veteran, Theologian, and Chief Servant of the Great King, who has Received many Revelations of Provable Truths from the Master Farmer, himself, whereby his many Good Books contain **"Guaranteed Solutions"** for our Massive Problems, including the Terrorist Attacks, Gang Wars, Drug Trafficking, Overdosing, Illegal Immigration, Refugees, Suicides, Vehicle Accidents, Wars, Abortions, Mass Shootings, needless Poverty, Crimes, Taxes, Loans, Interest Payments, etc., etc.! {See www.Amazon.com for: **"Guaranteed Solutions!" (HOW to Solve our Local and Global Problems in the Most Rational Manner Possible!) By The Worldwide People's Revolution!®, Book 080, plus: "All of the Arguments are in Favor of our Selected King, who has Zero Challengers!" (Before you Attend another Election Deception, you should Carefully Study this Inspired Book with an Honest Open Mind!) By The Worldwide People's Revolution!® Book 085.**}

00-07 [_] So, O Doctor Edison, is your Selected King some Kind of a Political Magician, or what? HOW in the World could anyone Devise a Plan whereby Terrorists would become Impotent? Does your Selected King not know that People can go Crazy at just any Time, and thus Do CRAZY Things — such as Crashing Vehicles into Crowds of Innocent People? {See: **"Terrorists Beware that your Days are Numbered!" (HOW to Bring those Terrorist Attacks to a Screeching HALT!) By The Worldwide People's Revolution!® Book 043.**}

00-08 [_] Well, that is the Reason that their Days are NUMBERED: beCause, once we get those **"GLORIOUS Swanky Hotels Castles and Fortresses"** BUILT, their Acts of Terrorism will CEASE for us Wise People, who Live within those **"Beautiful Planned City States for WISE Intelligent People with Common Sense and Good Understanding"**: beCause those Swanky Fortresses are easily Defended, being of *"First Class Quality,"* which is what *"Swanky"* Means. Therefore, when we Establish the New RIICHUS Wun-Werld GuvernMINT, all Aggressive Weapons will be done away with: beCause there will be no Need for them, since all "Enemies" will be Dethrone by **"The Swanky Sword of Divine Truths!" (The Most Powerful Weapon in the Whole Universe!) By The Worldwide People's Revolution!® Book 067.** Yes, it is all

Explained in the above mentioned Books. Therefore, I Strongly Suggest that you Study them, if you have not already done so. After all, God did NOT Die, and the one and only Way to be Liberated from the Prison of Lies is by Means of Learning the Truths that can Liberate us! Yes, Jesus said, *"You shall Learn the Truths that shall make you Free when you Practice them."* — *New MAGNIFIED Version (NMV)*

00-09 [_] So, O Doctor Sam, just Exactly what IS Swankynomics?

00-10 [_] Well, that is Thoroughly Explained in Chapter 01.

00-11 [_] O Doctor Sam, I do not Like the Idea of Living within a PRISON with Tall Stone Walls around it, which you call "Swanky FORTRESSES."

00-12 [_] Well, you only need to Study the following Drawings, which Reveal HOW to have FREE Electricity for everyone — Thanks to those Tall Stone Walls! And that is just ONE of many Great Advantages for them! For Example, they Keep OUT all of those Unwanted Varmints, which will Save TRILLIONS of Dollars over enough Time. For Example, I had a Naaber who Lost his entire Patch of Sweet Corn to a Hungry Family of Raccoons, while he was attending Church Services, and Praying to God for Help! Just Ask the Victims of Mass Shootings what they might Think about those Tall Stone Walls? Ask the Victims of Horrible Vehicular Accidents, if they would not rather be Living within those **"Beautiful Swanky PALACES!" (A New Concept in Living Habits — Swanky Palaces for Poor People!) By The Worldwide People's Revolution!®**, Book 066, which use Electric Elevators and Quiet Subway Trains, which are always on Time, without any Traffic Jams, Pollution, Accidents, nor Endless Transportation Costs?

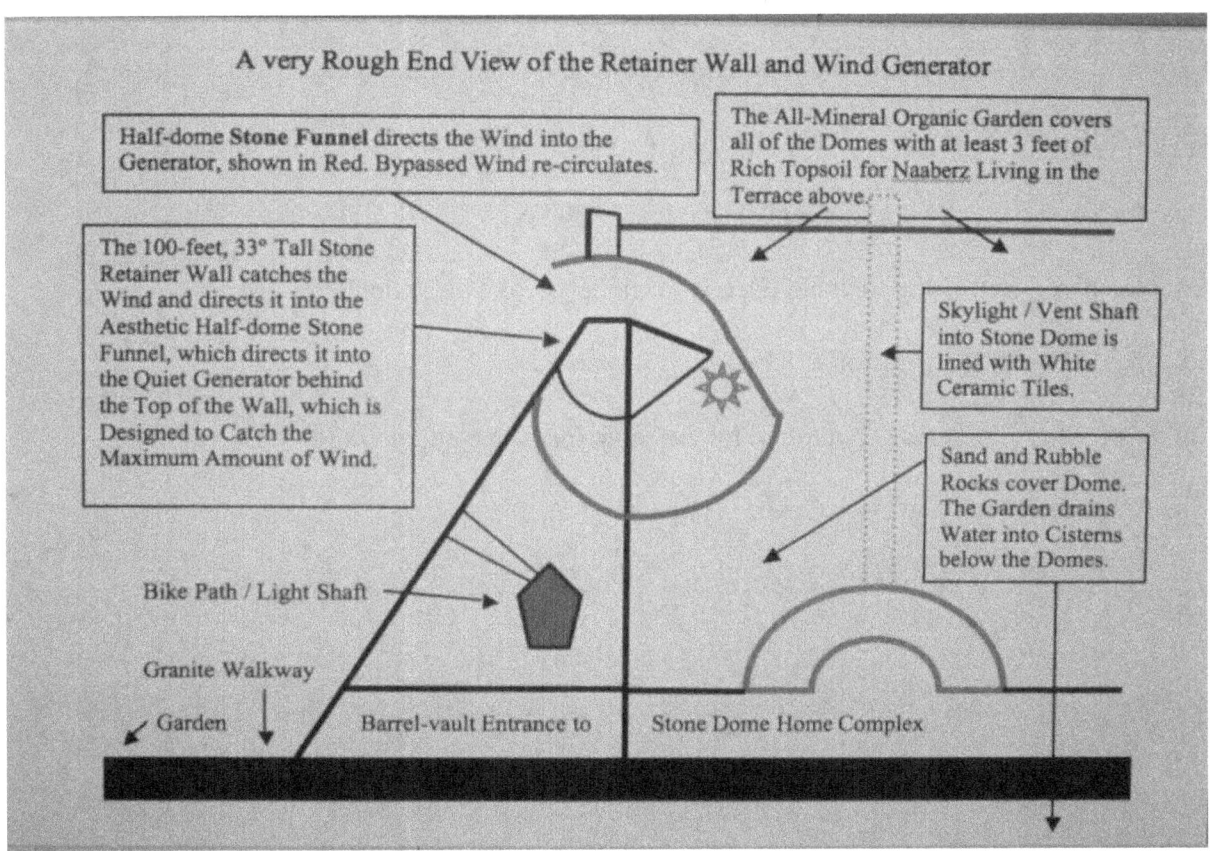

The Menu for a Feast of Provable Truths

Chapter 01 — What IS Swangkeenomiks? ... page 7

Chapter 02 — Is Swangkeenomiks Good for Everyone? ... 16

Chapter 03 — Did any other Society ever Practice Swangkeenomiks? ... 24

Chapter 04 — Swangkeenomiks is Biblical! ... 31

Chapter 05 — Swangkeenomiks Rules the Roost! ... 33

Chapter 06 — Swangkeenomiks has NO Competition! ... 35

Chapter 07 — Will Swangkeenomiks Eliminate Homelessness? ... 40

Chapter 08 — Will Swangkeenomiks Provide Free Health Care Insurance? ... 42

Chapter 09 — Swangkeenomiks Requires Money, and LOTS of it! ... 44

Chapter 10 — Will Swangkeenomiks Produce Greedy Selfish People? ... 49

Chapter 11 — Will Swangkeenomiks CRASH the Great False Economy? ... 52

Chapter 12 — An Explanation of the Cover Photo and Page 3 Photograph ... 67

Chapter 13 — Is Swangkeenomiks the Best Way to Exercise our Faith in God? ... 69

Chapter 14 — Does Swangkeenomiks Demand HONESTY? ... 74

Chapter 15 — Will Honest People Escape from the Great Tribulation? ... 77

Chapter 16 — The Conclusion ... 81

A List of other Fascinating Literature by the same Inspired Author ... 84

The Enticement is on the Back Cover ... page 95

This Book contains about 52,000 Words and 4 Photographs, counting the Cover Photo.

(HOW all People can Prosper in a RIIT WAA, and Stop Polluting the Earth with Capitalist TRASH!)

— Chapter 01 —

What IS Swangkeenomics?

01-01 [_] "Swangkeenomics" comes from 2 Basic Words — Swanky and Economics — and the Swanky is spelled in "Funetik Ingglish," which is one Way to Spell one Sound. For Example, in Standard Non-phonetic English, there are about 20 Different Ways to Spell the single Sound of "OO," as in sch**oo**l, r**u**le, d**o**, thr**ough**, sh**oe**, tw**o**, cr**ew**, fr**ui**t, r**hu**barb, r**heu**matism, rendezv**ous**, **Siou**x, L**ou**isiana, **ghou**l, pros**ciut**to, **lieu**, and p**ooh**: beCause that is the Barbarian Way that People have been doing it for hundreds of Years, in order to make it Difficult for Children to "Lern how tq reed and riit": beCause certain People stand to Gain a LOT of Money by our Ignorance, which might be Good for THEM; but, not for US. For Example, how many School Teachers would be Needed, if Children could Learn HOW to Read and Type Words at Home within a Day or 2: beCause of Wisely Using Computers as Teachers, Professors, and Educators? Indeed, each Sound can have just one or 2 Letters to Represent it, and Consistently so every Time. For Example, the simple letter "Q" could take the place of all of those **bold letters** in the words above here. {See www.Amazon.com for: **"The Public School of IGNERUNT FQLZ!" (HOW we have been GRAATLEE DISEEVD by Capitalism!)**, Book 024, plus: **"Are you a Jobless Graduate of the SKQL uv FQLZ?" (HOW to Get a GOUD EJUKAASHUN without Robbing the Bank!) By The Worldwide People's Revolution!®** Book 020.}

01-02 [_] O Selected King of **The Worldwide People's Revolution!®**, I always wondered just *why* the same sounds were spelled differently in books; but, now I understand that someone profits by it. Indeed, school teachers must earn their living somehow. Otherwise, what in the world would they do for an income? Would you Actually Want to Eliminate their JOBS? †§‡

01-03 [_] Well, in a Great False Economy, like our own, a Person is Reduced to the Value of a Tax Slave, you might say, who must go Looking for a JOB in the Sewage Pipes of Capitalism, at the Bottom Rung of the Economic Ladder, and Pray to some God that he or she will Discover such a Job before he or she becomes a Beggar on the Streets: beCause the following Economic Verse cannot be Found within the *Holy Bible, Koran, the Book of Mormon,* nor in any other *Holy Books,* including the *Constitution for the United States of America,* which Sorely Lacks much Important Information — such as the Following *Scripture,* or *Sacred Writing,* which should be Inserted into ALL of those Books, and many more!

> A-[_] A Righteous GovernMINT simply Mints and/or Prints the Necessary NEW Money — not to give it away to Ignorant Fools, nor to put it in the Control of Greedy Bankers; but, in Order to Use that Money WISELY, in Order to HIRE whomever is Willing and Able to Learn and Work, in Order to Help Build Beautiful Planned City States, which are Designed for Eternal Employment for everyone, which Stonework will Represent that New Money, without any Loans, without any Interest / Usury, and without any Taxes: beCause Taxes are only Needed by WICKED Anti-Christ FALSE governments.

01-04 [_] Please Check any Boxes below with an X, which have Statements that you Agree with:

A-[_] Such an Economic System would Cause Great Inflation on our Money, which would Ruin our Great False Economy. †§‡

B-[_] That New Money with New Faces and Numbers has no Connection with our Phony Fiat Money: because it must be Earned by Honest Labor, which Stonework Represents that New Money, which makes it Good Money. Guaranteed!

C-[_] I cannot Believe my Ears! Are you saying, O Selected King, that there never was any Need for POVERTY: beCause a Righteous One-World Government would have an Unlimited Supply of New Money, which it uses Wisely for doing Good Works? Are you Suggesting that a RIICHUS GuvernMINT has an Unlimited Supply of GOOD Money, which must be Earned by HONEST LABOR? Would that not Cause Great INFLATION on our almost Worthless Money?

D-[_] There is no Connection between our Phony Fiat Money and that New Money, which must be Earned by Honest Labor, according to **"A List of FAIR Swanky Wages,"** Book 065, without any Loans, without any Usury, without any Taxes, and without any Inflation: beCause an Hour's Worth of Common Labor will always be Worth an Hour's Worth of Common Labor, Eternally! Therefore, the Paper Bill will read: WUN OWER uv KOMUN LAABER, etc., etc. Therefore, if you can Sew a Pair of Shoes together within one Hour, with Machines, then those Shoes should Cost whatever the Materials Cost, plus your Labor, plus the Costs of Transportation, plus a Fair Price for any "Overhead" Expenses — such as the Workshop, Electricity, and the Sewing Machines, themselves.

E-[_] The Sewing Machines can belong to the Nq Riichus Wun-Werld GuvernMINT, as well as the Workshops and Sales Shops, which are Designed to Endure for thousands of Years, which Good Government can Collect 10% of the Profits for Taxes on the Shoes that are Sold, in order to Cover the Costs of the Sewing Machines, Workshops, Sales Shops, Transportation, Electricity, and all other Expenses. After all, most of those Things can be made to Endure the Test of Time, and be made of Top Quality Materials, and also be Maintained by that New Righteous One-World Government, by Faithful Servants.

F-[_] I much Prefer to OWN my own Workshop, Sales Shop, Sewing Machines, and whatever I Want to Work with: because I can take Better Care of it than any Lazy Government SERVANTS, who are otherwise known as Government SLAVES. †§‡

G-[_] I much Prefer to Own nothing, except for my Comb and Toothbrush. Indeed, I will Work for Common Minimum Slave Wages, and be Happy to Live in a Used Van, down by the River of Filthiness, where I can go Fishing for Contaminated Fishes with Huck Finn and Nigger Jim, and thus Contract Cancers: because we have to Die somehow. †§‡

H-[_] I much Prefer to Live in a First Class Swanky PALACE, which you can read about in: **"The Environmentalists' Paradise!" (HOW almost Everyone could be Living in a Beautiful Manmade Paradise!) By The Worldwide People's Revolution!® Book 035.** Yes, we could Raise our Standard of Living by no less than a hundred Times with our Elected King's Plan: beCause it is Inspired by GOD, who is All that is GOOD, who Believes in True Justice for ALL Peoples, Worldwide! HallaluYAH! Praise YAH! †§‡

(HOW all People can Prosper in a RIIT WAA, and Stop Polluting the Earth with Capitalist TRASH!)

I-[_] I Prefer to Live just as I have been Living: beCause I see nothing WRong with our Economy, much less with our Environment. Indeed, there is no such a Thing as Global Warming, and the Arctic Ice is NOT Melting, and Cars are Holy Things, which will be in the Kingdom of God. Yes, Jesus will be riding around in a Stretched Limousine with Michael Jackson and Elvis Presley. Indeed, he will have a Fat Cuban Cigar in one Hand, and a Glass of Champaign in the other Hand, while Chatting with Franklin D. Roosevelt, Winston Smokes Cigars Alcoholic Churchill, Saint Joseph Stalin, and Saddam Insane Hussein: beCause Jesus is a Capitalist with Communist and Socialist Flavorings. †§‡§§

J-[_] I Prefer to Live in the Pristine Garden of Eden with Adam and Eve; but, that is no longer Possible: because we have TERRORISTS in this World of Woes, who will not let us Live in Peace. †‡ {See www.Amazon.com for: **"Terrorists Beware that your Days are Numbered!" (HOW to Bring those Terrorist Attacks to a Screeching HALT!) By The Worldwide People's Revolution!®** Book 043.}

K-[_] I Want to Live like Rich Movie Stars, and have all of the latest Capitalist Toys in my House and Yard, as well as all of the Drugs and Drinks that make them Happy: because the Life of Christ is NOT for me. Indeed, King Jesus would Envy those Movie Stars for their True Riches. And I am NOT Crazy. Please pass to me the N-P-K (NPK) Champaign. †§‡

L-[_] I Believe in the American Dream, whereby 1% of the People Obtains 90% of the Wealth, and have Incomes that are 400 to 500 Times more than their Work Slaves.

M-[_] My Dream Home can Burn Up within 20 Minutes; but, I have Fire Insurance. Therefore, I am not Worried about it. Besides that, I Love those Heating, Cooling and Repair Bills. Moreover, I am the Envy of the World, and my Children get all of the Exotic Drugs that they might Want, whereby they are all Healthy and Happy: because Good Health is Obtained by Consuming Drugs. Indeed, if you Doubt it, ask Huck Finn. †§‡§§ {See the above Link for: **"Did God or Satan Ordain Medical Doctors?" (Ask Huck Finn and/or Nigger Jim: because neither Tom Sawyer nor Judge Thatcher would Know!) By The Worldwide People's Revolution!®** Book 022.}

N-[_] I Want a LUSCIOUS All-Mineral Organic Garden, so that I might be able to Eat Foods that I can Trust: beCause I have no Idea what is Actually IN nor ON my Foods. {See: **"The LUSCIOUS All-Mineral Organic Method of Gardening!" (HOW to Grow DELICIOUS Satisfying Foods for Potential Kingz and Kweenz in Swanky PALACES!)**, Book 021, which is a Companion Book of: **"Orgimmick Gardening at its Best!" (HOW to Grow Delicious Satisfying Foods without a 10-Million-Dollar Investment!) By The Worldwide People's Revolution!®** Book 079.}

O-[_] I Prefer to Live within one of those **"GLORIOUS Swanky Hotels Castles and Fortresses!" (Beautiful Planned City States for WISE Intelligent Well-Educated People with Common Sense and Good Understanding!)**, Book 019: beCause there are more than 5,000 Good Reasons and Great Advantages for Living within such City States. {See the above Link for: **"The Right Design for Living!" (A List of Great Advantages for Living within Beautiful Planned City States!) By The Worldwide People's Revolution!®** Book 012.}

9

P-[_] People will never be Contented to Live such simple Lives, and do their own Gardening: beCause it is Difficult SWEATY Work, which is WHY most People Left their Farms, and Moved into HOLY Cities of Confusion: beCause they Wanted to Raise their Standards of Living, beginning with those CARS, whereby they can get to Work. And so what if 400,000+ of those Ignorant Fools Die in Accidents, Worldwide, while 20 Million are Committed to Hospitals? Medical Doctors also need Work and High Wages. Jesus Christ would be the First in Line to Buy his Rolls Royce Sports Car. Guaranteed! †§‡§§

Q-[_] Have you never Heard of **"Seven Great Armies of Working Soldiers!" (HOW to Provide a Way for Everyone to WORK: so as to Eliminate Poverty, Crimes, Drug Abuses, Prisons and Unnecessary Taxes!) By The Worldwide People's Revolution!®**, Book 015? Well, all such Working Soldiers will make it Possible for everyone to get Set Up on the Land, Properly: so as to make Living on the Land a JOY, instead of Drudgery, as it used to be during the Dark Ages. Indeed, if Things are Set Up Properly, Life can be a hundred Times Better than it Presently is for 99.999,999% of the Masses of People in this World of Woes, who are Deprived of Fresh Clean Air, Pure Living Water, Wholesome Natural Foods, Natural Clothing, Secure Houses, and all of the Wonderful Things that our Selected King Proposes, including Beautiful Cathedrals, Churches, Mosques, Synagogues, Temples, Theaters, Gymnasiums, Tennis Courts, Heated Swimming Pools, Ice Skating Rinks, Bowling Alleys, Game Rooms, Museums, and whatever People Want, which can be made Possible by VOTING for our Selected King. {See www.Amazon.com for: **"Mark Twain Races for the PRESIDENCY!" (The 2020 Presidential Candidates Desperately Need Some STRONG Undefeatable COMPETITION!), Book 033, plus: "The Swanky Associations of Working Soldiers!" (A Fascinating Collection of Various Kinds of Voluntary Working Soldiers!), Book 018, plus: "Poverty Hunger Riots Strikes Brutalities Election Deceptions and Civil Wars!" (The High Price that we Earthlings have Paid for Leaving the Good Land!) By The Worldwide People's Revolution!®** Book 014.}

R-[_] I am an Independent Jackass, who does not Believe in Cooperation with any Armies of Working Soldiers, even if they have an Unlimited Supply of Money to Work with, as well as an Unlimited Amount of Building Materials: because there has never been an Efficient Army of Working Soldiers: because Governments can never do Things as Well as Businessmen. For Example, when President John Kennedy Proclaimed that Americans had to Land a Man on the Moon before the Decade was out, and bring him back Home Safely, it Required Civilian Scientists to get the Job Done: beCause the Federal Government was not Able to get the Job Done. Therefore, they Hired Wernher Magnus Maximilian Freiherr von Braun, who was Kidnapped from among Adolf Hitler's Chief Scientists, who became America's Chief Rocket Scientist, who Published a Book in 1958, called: **"The Impracticality of Going to the Moon!"** Yes, he wrote that it would Require no less than 3 Rocket Launchers the Height and Size of the Empire State Building in New York City, just to get Up to the Moon, and Return from the Moon, having one Rocket Launcher on the Moon, itself: beCause the Moon also has Gravity, and one-sixth as much Gravity as the Earth has. Therefore, in Order to get a Spacecraft Launched from the Moon at 4,000 Miles per Hour (MpH), that Rocket Launcher would have to have half as much Rocket Fuel as would FILL the Empire State Building! Yes, Wernher von Braun was the Chief Scientist, who Knew what was Required for going to the Moon, and Returning

(HOW all People can Prosper in a RIIT WAA, and Stop Polluting the Earth with Capitalist TRASH!)

Safely. However, the Saturn V Rocket for the Apollo 11 Mission was not even one Third as BIG as the Empire State Building, which you can Discover in *Wikipedia,* if you care to Educate yourself. Therefore, what are the Chances of Men Landing on the Moon, and Departing from it without Following the RULES and Laws of PHYSICS? HOW did the Lunar Lander Module (the *Eagle*) Depart from the Moon at 4,000 MpH with only a 5-gallon Propane Tank of Rocket Fuel? See the Drawings of the Spacecraft in *Wikipedia,* and Believe your Eyeballs! WHERE was the Rocket Launcher on the Moon? WHERE was the Rocket Fuel for Departing from the Moon? HOW could you People be so Incredibly STUPID and Credulous? †§‡§§

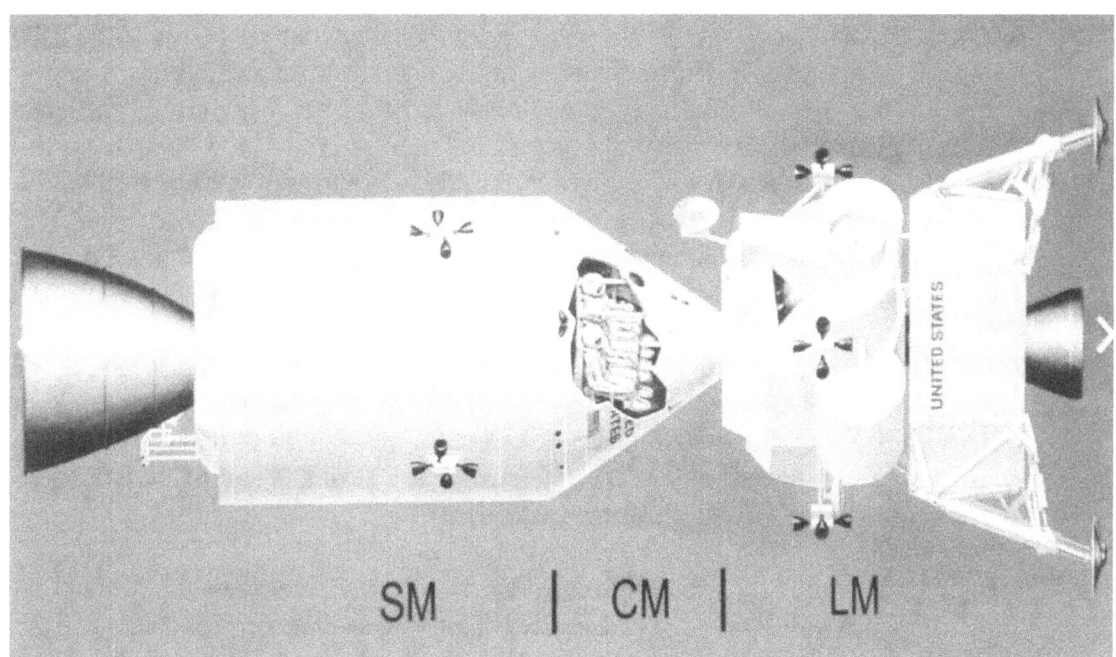

{FOOTNOTE: The Lunar Landing Module (LM) has no Space for a Million Gallons of Rocket Fuel for Departing from the Moon at 4,000 Miles per Hour (MpH). That is WHY it is called a HOAX — an All-American Federal Government HOAX! Stop and Think. That Contraption was not even Tested in the Realities of the Moon before it was used. It was the first Mechanical Device in all of History that Worked Perfectly the first time it was used. Thomas Edison would be Dumbfounded by it! He Experimented with some 3,000 Devices before he came up with a Workable Light Bulb. WHERE is the Rocket Fuel for it? WHERE is the Rocket Launcher for it on the Moon? 4,000 MpH is more than twice the Speed of a Bullet! Imagine a Bullet being Shot without a Barrel on the Weapon to Guide it in the Right Direction. The little Side Jets on the LM would hardly have any Effects when the Machine is going so Fast. Just Try sitting in such a Position for a Week. What if you got a Diarrhea? What if you Vomited inside of your Helmet on the Moon? What if the Radiation on the Moon Ruined your Kodak Film? What if you could not Stop the Wind from Blowing the Flag on the "Moon"? There are more than 100 Reasons WHY People did NOT Land on the Moon. Any one of those Reasons could Debunk the Hoax! Selah.}

S-[_] I say that Adolf Hitler had the most Efficient Army of Working Soldiers in all of History, who Mixed Up and Pour more Cubic Yards of Concrete within 6 Months, than 10

Times the Volume of the Great Pyramid in Egypt! (See the *History Channel* for the Proof.) Therefore, Working Soldiers can get a LOT of Work Done, if they are Inspired by a GOOD CAUSE. Yes, the Hoover Dam in Nevada is another Good Example of a Federal Government Project, which has Paid for itself many Times over by the ElecTrickery that it has Produced. {See www.Amazon.com for: **"UNLIMITED ENERJEE 99 Percent Pollutions Free!" (HOW to Obtain FREE ElecTrickery, Worldwide!)**, Book 029, plus: **"Does a Good Soldier have to be a MURDERER?" (Seven Great Swanky Armies of Voluntary Working Soldiers!) By The Worldwide People's Revolution!®** Book 027.}

T-[_] I say that Emperor Publius Aelius Hadrianus (General Hadrian) of Rome, who Lived from 24 January AD 76 to 10 July 138, was one of the Greatest Leaders of all Time, who Rebuilt the Pantheon, in Rome, with a Solid Concrete Roof, which has Stood Firm ever since then, and without any Rusty Steel Reinforcement Bars, which is Visited by more than 7 Million People per Year, and is a Mute / Silent Witness to the Great Accomplishments of Working Soldiers, even as the Great Pyramids in Egypt and Mexico are Mute Witnesses to what our Selected King Teaches — that Working Soldiers can Accomplish Great Things that Independent Jackasses can never Accomplish. Indeed, all of the Rich Capitalists in the World, combined, could never Afford to Build **"The Great World TEMPLE of PEACE,"** in Jerusalem, much less ONE GLORIOUS Swanky Castle, let alone a Swanky Fortress that is a hundred Miles in Diameter! Therefore, we must be WISE, and Establish the New RIGHTEOUS One-World GovernMINT. †‡ {See the above Link for: **"The CONSTITUTION for the New RIGHTEOUS One-World GovernMINT!" (HOW all Peoples can get True Justice, and Celebrate the Great Year of JUBILEE!) By The Worldwide People's Revolution!®** Book 016.}

U-[_] I Understand that there might be a Better Way to Live. However, I Seriously Doubt that Americans will Accept your Selected King's Master Plan: beCause most Americans are Fully Persuaded that Capitalism is the Financial Salvation of Mankind, in spite of Running at 90 Miles per Hour on a Dead End Street: beCause certain Natural Resources are Limited! †§‡ {See the above Link for: **"The Nature of CAPITALISM!" (A List of the EVILS of CAPITALISM!) By The Worldwide People's Revolution!®** Book 038.}

V-[_] I am Fully Persuaded that only Jesus Christ can Solve our Massive Problems, which will not be Solved until he Returns in all of his Naked Glory with his Holy Angels.

W-[_] The World is not Ready for the Dictatorship of Jesus Christ, who would have us Sleeping without Pillows. Indeed, he set a Good Example of his Tyrannical One-World Government, when he did not even Feed the Multitude who Followed him, until they had Starved for 3 Days, after Sleeping on the Grass by the Sea of Galilee. Moreover, he was the same Genocide Warlord who brought the Children of Israel out of Egypt, who Fed them with nothing but Boring Manna for 40 Years: beCause he was a TYRANT! See *First Samuel 15:3, King James Version (KJV)* for the Proof. †§‡

X-[_] X-amount of People have X-amount of Opinions, which they are Free to Express in: **"FREEDUM uv SPEECH!" (U Speshoul Maguzeen uv Onist Upinyunz!) By The Worldwide People's Revolution!®** Book 030-0002. {NOTE: His E-mail Address can be found in one of his Books for Serious Diligent Sincere Readers. See all Tables of Contents.}

(HOW all People can Prosper in a RIIT WAA, and Stop Polluting the Earth with Capitalist TRASH!)

Y-[_] I am Yearning for the Day of JUSTICE, when almost everyone in the World is Living within **"GLORIOUS Swanky Hotels Castles and Fortresses!" (Beautiful Planned City States for WISE Intelligent Well-Educated People with Common Sense and Good Understanding!) By The Worldwide People's Revolution!®**, Book 019, which will Solve ALL of our Massive Problems without any Tyrants in Charge: beCause no one will be FORCED to Say nor Do anything; but, they will be Fully Persuaded by Reason and Logic to Submit to **"The Swanky Sword of Divine Truths!"** Book 067. †§‡

Z-[_] The Zebras will never Agree to Cooperate: beCause they are very Stubborn Beasts. Moreover, we cannot Change the Leopard's Spots. Therefore, Swangkeenomiks will NOT Work. †§‡ {See: **"The Loathsome Burdens of the Independent Jackasses!" (A New Approach for Solving our Massive Problems!) By The Worldwide People's Revolution!®** Book 051.}

01-05 [_] O Selected King, are you Suggesting that the Verse of Scripture in Verse 01-03-A should have been put into all *Bibles, Korans, Books of Mormon,* and even Carved into Granite Stones within every Courthouse in the World: beCause, *"MONEY Answers all Questions,"* as King Solomon wrote in *Ecclesiastes 10:19?* Indeed, for a Lack of Money, Billions of People have Suffered for thousands of Years. Moreover, many People have been Murdered for their Money. In Fact, many People are now in Prisons for Seeking more Money, Illegally.

01-06 [_] Please Check the Boxes below with Statements that you Agree with:

A-[_] A Good Government would not Produce any Criminals of any Kind. Jesus Christ will not have Prisons when he Governs the World.

B-[_] Jesus Christ will Lock Satan up in a Prison: so that he cannot Tempt People to Sin for at least a thousand Years. (See *Revelation 20* in Chapter 11, Verse 12-K.)

C-[_] In the Real World, Satan is very much Alive and Well. Indeed, his Throne is on Wall Street in New Yuck City, which is Governed by Rich Edomite Bankers. †§‡

D-[_] A Good GovernMINT would Practice the Great Truth that is Taught in Verse 01-03-A, which any Intelligent 12-year-old Children can easily Understand. Indeed, if you Doubt it, just Ask them to Read it and Explain it to you. I Beg you, PLEASE Try it.

E-[_] God did not Intend that People should Build Beautiful Planned City States, much less Govern themselves According to their own Elected Laws and Flexible Rules: beCause that might Eliminate Confusion, which God LOVES. Remember the Tower of Babel. †§‡

F-[_] God Loves all of us, and HATES the Tower of Babel; but, we do not Love each other, or else we would Establish a NQ RIICHUS Wun-Werld GuvernMINT, which does what is RIIT for ALL of the People, including Black, Blue, Brown, Freckled, Gray, Green, Mulatto, Pink, Polka-dotted, Purple, Red, and White People. †§‡

G-[_] God only Loves those People who Love him, and none of them would even Touch that Filthy Money, which is the Root Cause for almost all of our Evils in this World of

Woes. †‡ {See www.Amazon.com **"For the Love of Money!" (The Strange Things that People Say and Do to Get more Money!)**, Book 003.}

H-[_] Money is only a Medium of Exchange for Goods and Services. Therefore, Money, itself, is no more Evil than Water nor Fire, which can Save you or even Kill you — Depending on HOW it is Used.

I-[_] Money cannot be Used Wisely. Ask King Solomon, if you Doubt it. †§‡ {See the above Link for: **"ECCLESIASTES UNCOVERED!" (The New MAGNIFIED Version of Ecclesiastes and the Song of Solomon in Plain English!)**, Book 034.}

J-[_] Freedom and Justice Demands that Money is Used Wisely, and ONLY Wisely. Indeed, the Government should Regulate it, and Use it Wisely for making all People Moderately Rich: so that no one is Lusting after it: beCause they have Plenty of it, which they have Earned by Honest Labor, without any Loans, without any Interest, and without any Taxes: because all such Healthy Happy People just Naturally LOVE their Good GovernMINT; and therefore, they Cheerfully GIVE whatever Money is Needed for Supporting such a Good Government, which is called a TITHE or OFFERING. ‡

K-[_] King Jesus would be Loved by all of the People: beCause he would make a Way for them to become Moderately Rich, just by their Labors, alone. Therefore, the People would Gladly Support his Holy Kingdom with their Tithes and Offerings.

L-[_] Lots of Laughs! King Jesus would be Assassinated by a Suicide Bomber the very First Day that he Sits on his Capitalist Paper-mache Throne: beCause of being put Out of Business by Swangkeenomiks. †§‡

M-[_] Money is the Answer for Solving the Poverty Problem. However, it is Better to Keep that Money in the Bank Vaults of Rich Red Jew Bankers: because we might Need that Money for Financing World War 3. †§‡§§

N-[_] Why not Mint and Print NEW Money with New FACES for Hiring **"Seven Great Armies of Working Soldiers"** to Help Build those **"GLORIOUS Swanky Hotels Castles and Fortresses,"** so as to Eliminate Poverty and Crimes, Worldwide, which is Swangkeenomiks in a Nutshell?

O-[_] Are there no OPTIONS? Will we have to Accept that New Octopus Concept in Economics, whereby the One-World Government OWNS all of the Property, and we Own nothing but our Tooth Brushes and Combs? How in the World could that be True Prosperity? Indeed, I Prefer an Oligarchy! ‡

P-[_] People have Instinctively Known for thousands of Years that there must be a Better Way to Live. However, being Poor with a Capital P — as in Mentally, Spiritually, Financially, Materially, and Physically POOR — they are not Able to Comprehend Swangkeenomiks: beCause of the Beauty of its Simplicity. After all, Greedy Bankers have made the Subject of Money Extremely Complicated, by Inventing Complexities. ‡

(HOW all People can Prosper in a RIIT WAA, and Stop Polluting the Earth with Capitalist TRASH!)

Q-[_] The Great Question is this: **"Will Humanity have to go on Suffering for another thousand Years for the LACK of MONEY?"** Just Answer that Question in your own Mind. Yes, STOP and THINK about it.

R-[_] Righteous People HATE Complications, Confusion, and Red Jew Scams. Bankers are NOT Needed for True Prosperity.

S-[_] Snakes are Needed in Hawaii to Eat Birds. †§‡

T-[_] People can Live Happily without Snakes, Skunks, Sneaky Spies, and Temptations.

U-[_] United Effort is the KEY to True Prosperity; but, without LOTS of Money to Work with, nothing can get Done. Therefore, Money is the Solution for that Problem, and Good Money should be Minted and Printed by the CONGRESS, according to our Constitution.

V-[_] To Hell with your Constitution. We Bankers are in Charge of the Money, and we will Determine WHO gets any of it, whereby WE can Control the Great False Economy, and Finance both Sides of every War, and thus Get much Richer by it. Indeed, when a War gets going, the Federal Government MUST have Money, which only comes from us Edomite Bankers: beCause we are in Charge of it. Period. †§‡§§

W-[_] Wars are Orchestrated by False Governments, who Borrow much Money from Red Jew Bankers, which has to be Repaid with Interest / Usury: because Bankers are Worthy of LOTS of Money, while Poor Farmers in Guatemala are Unworthy of any Money, even to Build Good Houses for themselves, much less, **"Beautiful Swanky PALACES!"** †§‡§§

X-[_] X-amount of People, like Bonnie Parker and Clyde Barrow, Agree with you, and therefore they become Bank Robbers. However, no one should have to become a Criminal, just to get Enough Money to Work with. Therefore, we Need to Establish a NQ RIICHUS Wun-Werld GuvernMINT, which can be Proven in a Courtroom. ‡

Y-[_] It might have been a Good Idea during Yesteryears; but, now it is too Late. Indeed, the Earth is almost Ruined by Capitalist PIGS, who are still Selling Pesticides, Herbicides, Toxic Paints, Solvents, and all Kinds of Poisonous Harmful Chemicals, Drugs, and Abominations. †§‡ {See www.Amazon.com for: **"The Nature of CAPITALISM!"** (A List of the EVILS of CAPITALISM!) By The Worldwide People's Revolution!® Book 038.}

Z-[_] The ZEAL of our Selected King will Straighten us Out: beCause he is the Man with the Spirit of Elijah! (See *Malachi 4* in any *Bible*.)

01-07 [_] O Selected King, is that True? Are you the Man with the Spirit of Elijah? Will you Command Fire to come down from the Sky and Consume **"The BIG White OUTHOUSE on the Not-so-Biblical Capitol DUNGHILL!"**?

01-08 [_] Well, if that is what is Required for Straightening those Wicked Politicians Out, then so be it.

01-09 [_] Can we not Settle our Differences in a Civilized Way, without going to War with GOD?

01-10 [_] Well, we could, just by DEMANDING "**The GREAT Worldwide TELEVISED Court HEARING!" (That Great Meeting of the Most Intelligent and Well-Educated Minds!) By The Worldwide People's Revolution!®** Book 041. However, the Vast Majority of the People have never Heard of Swangkeenomiks. Therefore, they have no Idea what they are Missing! ‡

— Chapter 02 —

Is Swangkeenomiks Good for Everyone?

02-01 [_] Well, if anyone Objects to the Idea of almost everyone in the World becoming Moderately Rich, then Swangkeenomiks might not be Good for them, who are Welcome to Live with Huck Finn and Nigger Jim down by the River of Filthiness in their Used Rusty Van. Indeed, it could be that they Need to Suffer Longer in their Confused State of Extreme Poverty: beCause of not coming to their Right Senses with the Prodigal Son of *Luke 15*. {See: **"The New MAGNIFIED Version of the GOOD NEWS According to Saint LUKE!" (The Magnified Gospel of Luke in Plain English!) By The Worldwide People's Revolution!®** Book 061.}

02-02 [_] O Selected King of **The Worldwide People's Revolution!®**, I have no Idea who the Prodigal Son was, and I am far too Lazy to look it up in any *Bible*. In Fact, I do not even have a *Bible* in the House.

02-03 [_] Well, the Internet has many Bibles: beCause it is the single most-sold and Studied Book in the World. Search for the *Blue Letter Bible,* which has many Versions, including the New MAGNIFIED Version in Plain English, which is the most Popular Version by a hundred Times! But, if you Doubt it, just Read it Carefully: beCause it is the one and only Version that is Inspired by the Most High God, which can be Proven in a Courtroom with Law and Order. For Example, in the Beginning, one of the Gods said to the other Gods, *"Let us make Mankind in our Images, according to our own Likenesses, and let them have Dominion over all of the Earths that we have Created for them, whereby we can Discover the Best Spirits among them, and thus make them the Supreme Rulers of their own New Worlds, which are continually being Born in the Nebulas, who will otherwise be known as Gods. After all, there are Billions of Trillions of Worlds to be Inhabited by People, Animals, and Plants of Various Kinds, who Need Gods to Govern them in a Riit Waa, whereby they can make those Worlds very Beautiful Peaceful Places for everyone to Live, if they Love and Obey their Great Creator Gods."* And thus Jesus Christ was found Worthy to Govern this World of Wonders: beCause he Proved himself to be a Better Spirit than all of the others, even in another World of a Higher Order than this World, whose Chosen Disciples were also Proven to be Better Spirits than most People, except for that Judas Iscariot, who Proved himself to be a Betrayer of Trust, and thus a Son of Satan — all for the Love or Lust for Money, which is the Root Cause for almost all Evils. †§‡ {See: **"The Root Cause for almost all Evils!" (The Strange Things that People Say and Do to Get more Money!) By The Worldwide People's Revolution!®**, Book 078, which is a Companion Book of: **"For the Love of Money!"** Book 003.}

(HOW all People can Prosper in a RIIT WAA, and Stop Polluting the Earth with Capitalist TRASH!)

02-04 [_] O Elected King of **"The New RIGHTEOUS One-World Government,"** why do you not just take the Time to Quote *Luke 15?* After all, it cannot be all that Long: because Jesus never gave any LONG Parables, nor even Wrote any Books: because his Carpenter Hands were Awkward. †§‡

A-[_] And Jesus said, "A certain Man had 2 Sons, and the Younger one said to his Father, 'Please give to me the Portion of my Inheritance from you: because I want to See the World before I get Old and Helpless, like you, and Unable to See it.' And thus the Father Divided unto his 2 Sons his Inheritance, by Selling his Livestocks, and giving the Money to his Younger Son, while giving his Property to his Oldest Son, who continued to Manage it.

B-[_] "And, not many Days after that, the Younger Son gathered up his Personal Belongings, and took his Journey into a far away Country: because he had Heard that Life was Better over there; but, it was not long before he had Wasted all of his Substance with Riotous Living with Ignorant Fools. And thus, when he had Spent all of it, there arose a Terrible Famine in that Land of Shame: because the Rain had Stopped; and thus he began to be in Want for the Necessities of Life. Therefore, he went to another Country, and Joined himself to a certain Citizen of that Country, who raised Various Kinds of Swines, who sent him into the Fields to Gather Corn for the Hogs, who were Living under Sheds in Pig Pens. Indeed, that Man was Generous, and Offered to him all of the Corn that he might Want to Eat in the Field; but, after a Month or so of Eating that Corn, it became Loathsome to him, whereby he just Naturally Lost his Appetite for it.

C-[_] "Then it came to pass that he got Hungry, after not Eating for many Days, whereupon even the Corn Husks looked Appetizing to him: because he had an Intense Appetite; but, all of the Corn was gone, and only the Husks were left with the Filthy Hogs, who were Wallowing in the Mud, who were Meditating on Eating him: because they were also Hungry. Indeed, you can tell by the Looks in their Eyes. However, the Boy did not venture into the Pens with the Swines: because he could Sense the Danger of it.

D-[_] "And it came to pass that the Boy went to Sleep, and had a Dream about Eating a large Thanksgiving Meal at his Father's House; and thus he Awoke and came to his Right Senses, and said to himself: 'How many Hired Servants of my Father's Household have such a Miserable Life as I have? Indeed, they have Plenty of Foods to Eat, and enough Spare Foods to Feed the Beggars, while I am about to Perish with Hunger! Therefore, I will Arise and go to my Father, and I will say to him: "Father, I have Sinned against the God of Heaven, and have done a Great Injustice to you, also; and therefore, I am no more Worthy to be called your Son; but, please make me as one of your Hired Servants: because I have been a Fool, even a Great Ignorant FOOL!"'

E-[_] "And thus he Arose, and came to his Father with his Skin and Bones: because his Flesh had Vanished during the Great Famine. However, when he was still a long way off, and barely able to Walk for his Weakness, his Father saw him Coming slowly toward him, walking with a Stick for a Cane to Steady himself, lest he should Faint and Fall on his Face, and the Father Recognized his Tattered Cloak by its Colors; and thus he had Compassion on him, and Ran to Greet him, and fell on his Neck, and Kissed him, and Hugged him, and Cried on him for the Space of an Hour or more; and when his Son finally brought himself around to where he could stop Weeping on his Father, he said to him: 'Father, I have Sinned against the God of Heaven, and in your Sight, also: because I have done a Great Injustice to you by Wasting your Inheritance to Waste on Harlots; and therefore, I am no longer Worthy to be called your Son. Therefore, Please make me as one of your Servants.'

F-[ ] "However, the Father said to his Servants, 'Take this Poor Lad to the Shower House, and give to him a Bath and a Shower, and bring forth the Best Clean White Robe, and put it on him, and Anoint his Head with Fragrant Oil, and put a Ring on his Finger, and Shoes on his Feet: because he has Repented, and come Home to his Father. Yes, bring here the Fatted Calf, also, and Kill it for a Feast; and let us all Eat and be Merry: because this, my Son, was Spiritually Dead in Trespasses and Sins; but, now he is Alive, once again; yes, he was Lost in the Darkness of Ignorance, like a Sheep who Wandered Astray; but, now he has Seen the Light of Truths, and is Found by the Good Shepherd, who Lives in the Heaven above, in the Secret City of the Great King.' And thus they began to make themselves Merry with a Bottle of Wine. {See www.Amazon.com for: **"The Secret City of the Great King!" (HOW the True Church will Escape from the Great Tribulation!) By The Worldwide People's Revolution!® Book 042.**}

G-[ ] "Now, it came to pass that the Elder Son was not at Home at the Time; but, he was Busy in the Lower Field, on the Backside of the Farm; and as he came Walking from the Field, and drew near to the House, he Heard Music and the Sound of People Dancing and making themselves Merry; and thus, while he was still in the Barn, attending to his Oxens, he called one of the Servants, and asked what the Meaning of all of the Noise was about?

H-[ ] "And the Servant said to him, 'Your Brother has come Home; and your Father has Killed the Fattened Calf: because he has Received him Safe and Sound, after Worrying over him for so Long, which made his Hairs Gray, and his Heart Broken; but, now he is a Happy Father, once again.'

I-[ ] "And thus the Elder Son became Angry, and would not go into the House. Therefore, the Father came out, and Entreated him to come in. But, he said to his Father, 'Look here, Old Man, I have Served you for all these many Years, and have Loved you much more than my Brother; neither did I Transgress your Commandments at any Time; and yet you never gave to me so much as a Kid Goat for a Feast, so that I might make myself Merry with my Friends. However, as soon as this Whoremonger, your Younger Son, has come Home, who has Devoured your Living with Prostitutes and Drunkards, you have Killed for him the Fattened Calf, and brought out the Best Wine, and Dressed him with a Clean White Robe, and put a Silver Ring on his Finger, and Anointed his Head with Fragrant Oil — even according to all that the Servant told me, right?'

J-[ ] "And the Father said to him, 'O my Son, please do not be Angry with me: because you are forever with me, and all that I Possess will be yours when I am gone. Indeed, it was Fitting and Proper that we should make ourselves Merry, and be very Glad for your Brother: because he was as good as Dead, and is Alive once again. Yes, he was Lost like an Innocent Lamb in a Wilderness of Sins with Wild Beasts all about; but, now he has been Found by the Holy Angels, and brought back Home to the Loving Arms of his Compassionate Father. Therefore, come into the House, and fall on his Neck and Kiss him and Hug him: because he is your only Little Brother, who is now little more than Skin and Bones: because of the Great Famine in that Shameful Land, which Killed thousands of People. Therefore, let us be most Thankful for all that we have: because Things could be a lot Worse than they are for us.' And thus he went into the House, and fell on his Brother's Neck, and Kissed him, and Hugged him, and Cried on him, and Confessed to him that he must have been a Bad Example for him to Follow, or else he would have never Left his Home on the Farm, to Wander into some City of Confusion with Hordes of Ignorant Fools, who were Deprived of Good Understanding and True Wisdom, who did not even have a Good Supply of Foods and Water, who were not Prepared for the Worst Conditions that Nature might bring onto them, who Trusted in Lady Luck to Save them, rather than get their Lazy Asses Out of Bed and Build Beautiful Planned City States for themselves."

01-[_] I Cried when I Heard that Story.

02-[_] I did NOT Cry.

03-[_] I wanted to Cry; but, for some Strange Reason my Well of Tears was already Dry. Indeed, it is Obvious that my Heart has been Hardened like a Stone that is Under the Pressure of a Mountain of Debts, whereby I have become Cold and Spiritually Dead, being without any Empathy, nor even Sympathy.

04-[_] You must Humble yourself by Means of Fasting and Praying, until your Heart Softens up, and your Spirit comes back to Life with the Prodigal Son.

K-[_] I Freely Confess that King Jesus tells the Best of Good Stories. However, I could tell my own Stories about the Drudgeries on the Farm, and how we put in 16-hour Days, and how God Rained Down Hailstones to Wipe Out our Crops, and Lightning to Burn Up our Fields and Forests, and Worms to Ruin our Fruits, and thus make Life Miserable for all of us; but, who would Care to Listen to all such Stories? ‡

L-[_] Lots of Laughs! — you do not even know what it Means to Suffer in a War, whereby you might get 2 or 3 Hours of Sleep per Day, and Wade around in the Mud, and have your Feet and Crotch Rot with Jungle Rot, and have to Listen to the Bombs Bursting all Night, while being so Depressed by it all that you Wish to God that one of those Bombs might Fall on you, and thus get Rid of you! Yes, you may Blame it onto Fascism, Capitalism, Socialism, Communism, or whatever you like; but, in all Cases, it is the Fault of those Lying Conniving Edomites, who Deliberately take Advantage of Poor Ignorant People. †‡

M-[_] I say that the Father was not very Wise, or else he would not have Spoiled his Boy with so much Money at one Time, whereby he made a Fool of himself for his Pride. ‡

N-[_] Not everyone has a Rich Father with a Good Inheritance; but, Young Men often Join the Army, and make Drunken Fools of themselves during the Weekends: beCause of having the same Lusts and Longing Desires that the Younger Son had, who should have been Married, and Living at Home on the Farm.

O-[_] Well, that is just your Honest Opinion. However, I say that he Needed a Righteous Government, which Owns all of the Lands, Houses, Building Materials, Money, and everything: beCause it was his Inheritance that Corrupted him, which is another Red Jew Idea, which would not be Possible with a Righteous Government, which would see to it that everyone is Moderately Rich, having a Good Secure House to Live in, which is Fireproof, Mouse-proof, Rat-proof, Hail-proof, Tornado-proof, Hurricane-proof, Flood-damage-proof, Termite-proof, Rot-proof, Paint-proof, Insurance-proof, and Self-air-conditioned, having Polished Marble Walls, Granite Floors, Agate Windows, a large million-gallon Cistern for Water Storage, a Luscious All-Mineral Organic Garden, Vineyard, and Orchard, being Attached to a Walk-in Cooler / Freezer / Root Cellar / Pantry, and a Spacious Kitchen and Dinning Room, which is Attached to a large Living Room Dome, Bedroom Domes with Spacious Bathrooms, and all of that Complex Attached to the Home-craft Workshop with Well-made Tools, which is Attached by a Wide Tunnel to the Sales Shop with Polished Marble Walls, having Skylight Holes and Windows in every Stone Dome Home Complex for Fresh Clean Air: beCause all of those Good Things are Possible, and most Practical, now that we have Mechanical Slaves for doing all of the Difficult Labor. ‡ {See www.Amazon.com for: **"The Environmentalists' Paradise!" (HOW almost Everyone could be Living in a Beautiful Manmade Paradise!) By The Worldwide People's Revolution!®**, Book 035, which is a Companion Book of: **"Beautiful Swanky PALACES!" (A New Concept in Living Habits — Swanky Palaces for Poor People!) By The Worldwide People's Revolution!®** Book 066.}

P-[_] Talk about a Paradise — you forgot to Mention that each Family Stone Dome Home Complex would be Connected with the Swanky PALACE, which would have all of those Good Things that are Mentioned in Verse 01-04-Q. Moreover, if a Person has not Studied your other Wonderful Books, O Elected King, they might not Understand that all of those Self-air-conditioned Stone Dome Home Complexes would have those Luscious All-Mineral Organic Gardens on their ROOFS: so that the Family who Lives ABOVE them in the next Terrace, would have their Garden Directly in Front of their House, even as your own Garden would also be Directly in Front of your own House: so that you would not have to be going Up the Electric Elevator, just to get to your Garden.

Q-[_] The Great Question is this: **"Does God Love Swangkeenomiks, whereby no one Owns anything except for his or her Personal Belongings** — such as Clothing, Bathroom Items, Books, CD's and DVD's? Indeed, with Swangkeenomiks, one does not Own very much; but, one gets to Live his or her Life in a Swanky PALACE, instead of in a Used Rusty Van down by the Filthy River with Fat Farley. In Fact, all such Wise People would be Living like Kings and Queens in **"Beautiful Swanky PALACES,"** IF they just Learned, Believed, Loved, and OBEYED *the New MAGNIFIED Version of the 20 Commandments,* which you can find in: **"LIGHTNING STRIKES Versus Lightning Bugs!" (HOW you can Become Moderately RICH, without Telling any Lies nor Selling any Trash!) By The Worldwide People's Revolution!®**, Book 074, which is one of the most Powerful and Persuasive Books in the Whole World! Guaranteed!

R-[_] The Proof that God does Love Swangkeenomiks is found in the Fact that all of Nature Practices it — at least concerning Ownership of Things: beCause no Wild Animal OWNS anything, nor are any of them Possessed by the Evil Spirit of GREED. Yes, some of them are Selfish for Survival Reasons; but, none of them are Greedy, and none of them Horde up Wealth for themselves, like People do. †‡

(HOW all People can Prosper in a RIIT WAA, and Stop Polluting the Earth with Capitalist TRASH!)

S-[_] So, if no one Owns anything, except for their Toothbrush and Comb, you might say, what would be the Incentive for getting Out of Bed in the Morning? Indeed, who would have any Interest in going to Work? What would be the Motive for doing anything?

T-[_] The Incentive or Motive would be to Live like a King or Queen in a Swanky PALACE, instead of Living as Education Slaves, Work Slaves, Tax Slaves, Interest Slaves, Insurance Slaves, Rent Slaves, Food Bills Slaves, and Endless Bills Slaves in Wooden / Plastic Firetrap Mouse-infested Cockroach Dens, which have Eternal Repair Bills to Pay, Heating and Cooling Bills, Electric Bills, Mortgage Payments, Property Taxes, etc., etc.

U-[_] I Understand how Nice it would be IF Swangkeenomiks became a Reality; but, with Satan still Roaming all about, what are the Chances of it becoming a Reality?

V-[_] We, the People, have to make it become a Reality, by DEMANDING "**The GREAT Worldwide TELEVISED Court HEARING,**" whereby we might Persuade almost everyone in the Whole World to Sacrifice their PRIDE, and Humble themselves by Means of Fasting and Praying, until their Nostrils and Taste Buds are Working Properly, and then Establish "**The New RIGHTEOUS One-World Government,**" whereby we can all get Out of our Confounded States of Extreme Poverty, and end up Living in those "**GLORIOUS Swanky Hotels Castles and Fortresses!**" — even within **Beautiful Planned City States for WISE Intelligent Well-Educated People with Common Sense and Good Understanding! By The Worldwide People's Revolution!® Book 019.**

W-[_] Well, that is the Box that I Checked with an X: beCause, unless the Masses of People in this World of Wonders should LEARN all about our Selected King's Master Plan, there is no Way that we are going to end up Living in "**The Environmentalists' Paradise!**" **(HOW almost Everyone could be Living in a Beautiful Manmade Paradise!)**, Book 035. And the Option is to Suffer with more and more Terrorist Attacks, School Shootings, Mass Murders, Tornado Insanities, Hurricane Destructions, Earthquake Disasters, House Fires, and perhaps with World War 3! Yes, the Punishment for Rejecting such Enlightening Truths is the Great Tribulation, which could End with a Great Atomic NIGHTMARE! Therefore, it is now Time to Act WISELY. {See www.Amazon.com for: "**Terrorists Beware that your Days are Numbered!**" **(HOW to Bring those Terrorists Attacks to a Screeching HALT!) By The Worldwide People's Revolution!® Book 043.**}

X-[_] X-amount of People will Believe and Obey, while X-amount will NOT Believe nor Obey: beCause that is the Nature of Human Beings. However, there is Overwhelming Evidence to Prove that Capitalism is Running on a Dead-end Street: beCause there are Limited Natural Resources. Therefore, when those Resources RUN OUT, we will all be in BIG TROUBLE: beCause a Gallon of Gas will Cost 100$, or more! Therefore, Nature, itself, will FORCE US TO CHANGE OUR WAYS! Yes, Climate Changes will also FORCE US TO RETHINK OUR PHONY EDOMITE CAPITALIST LIFESTYLE. {See the above Link for: "**HOW to Prepare for CLIMATE CHANGES!**" **(The Wisest Plan for Mankind to Follow!), Book 004, plus: "The Nature of CAPITALISM!" (A List of the EVILS of CAPITALISM!) By The Worldwide People's Revolution!® Book 038;** and Understand, O Sinners, that we must STOP Sinning, in Order to be Saved.}

Y-[_] You might Imagine that I do not Believe in your Selected King's Master Plan; but, it is my Wife who does not Believe, and I do not Want to Offend her by Confessing the Whole Truth about ALL Important Subjects: beCause she is a Highly-Perfumed Painted SKUNK, you might say, who has Big Breasts to Suck on, which I am Addicted to, not to Mention her other Fascinating Parts; and her Brother is a Lying Edomite Snake, who Wears a Multi-Colored Coat of Self-Deceptions, who Strikes at the Colorful Peacock from Angel Ridge with his Poisonous Fangs of Hate and Revenge: beCause his Inspired Words of Provable Truths put him Out of Business, which is the Business of Preaching Outlandish LIES! {See: **"An Amazing Collection of Wit and Wisdom!" (The Marvelous Tale of the Colorful Peacock from Angel Ridge, and the Strong Rope of Everlasting Hope!) By The Worldwide People's Revolution!® Book 048.**}

Z-[_] So, you must be a ZEBRA, who is neither Hot nor Cold toward the Truth. Therefore, there will be no Place for you within the Holy Kingdom of the Gods, unless you REPENT. {See: **"HOW to Become a HOLY Man!" (40 Good Reasons WHY People Should FAST and PRAY!), Book 045, which is a Companion Book of: "The Proper RULES for FASTING!" (The Complete Instruction Manual for True Repentance!) By The Worldwide People's Revolution!® Book 046.**}

02-05 [_] I would say that Swangkeenomiks would be Good for everyone, if they could come to Realize just how many Great Advantages there are for Accepting it, which might seem to be Painful, at first; but, once everyone has Settled Down in their **"Beautiful Swanky PALACES,"** they will be quite Happy with them, even as the Pope of Rome is quite Happy in his Palace, and even as all Presidents are Happy to Live in their Palaces, which few of them OWN. After all, they will get to Drink lots of Fresh Sweet Natural Fruit Juices, which Poor Miserable People cannot Afford, nowadays, which will be Encouraging to them: beCause such Juices are called *"the Waters of Life,"* in the *Scriptures*. Indeed, such Fresh Fruit Juices make you Feel ALIVE! {See: **"The LUSCIOUS All-Mineral Organic Method of Gardening!" (HOW to Grow DELICIOUS Satisfying Foods for Potential Kingz and Kweenz in Beautiful Swanky PALACES!) By The Worldwide People's Revolution!®, Book 021, which is a Companion Book of: "Did God or Satan Ordain Medical Doctors?" (Ask Huck Finn and/or Nigger Jim: because neither Tom Sawyer nor Judge Thatcher would Know!), Book 022, which is a Companion Book of: "Orgimmick Gardening at its Best!" (HOW to Grow Delicious Satisfying Foods without a 10-Million-Dollar Investment!) By The Worldwide People's Revolution!®, Book 079.** However, if those Books sound Boring to you, perhaps you should Study: **"The BIG White OUTHOUSE on the Not-so-Biblical Capitol DUNGHILL!" (The Chief Sins of the Divided States of United Lies!), Book 023,** which tells all about that Stinking Outhouse, which has the 2 very Odious Holes for the Dimwitcrats and Reprobates to Squat on, which Stinks from the Top to the Bottom with Ancient Elephant Droppings and Fresh Political Donkey Dung: beCause of having Diarrheas of their Minds, whereby their Mouths are Running much of the Time, in spite of Suffering with Chronic Constipation of their Minds, whereby they cannot Understand **"The New MAGNIFIED Version of the Book of ACTS!" (The Understandable Version of the ACTS of the Apostles in Plain English!), Book 063,** which Explains what it Means to have *"... all Things in Common ..."* Indeed, all True Christians will LOVE IT: beCause it Explains HOW they can all become Moderately RICH, and without Telling any Lies, nor Selling any Capitalist TRASH — much less make SLAVES of themselves for some Evil Empire of Wicked Edomites, who are like those Egyptian Task Masters in *the Book of Exodus!*}

(HOW all People can Prosper in a RIIT WAA, and Stop Polluting the Earth with Capitalist TRASH!)

02-06 [_] O Elected King of **The Worldwide People's Revolution!®**, are you not Afraid of Stirring Up the Hornet's Nest called CAPITALISM, whereby those Rich Greedy Hornets will be Swarming and Attacking you from all Sides: beCause of Speaking Evil of their Economic GODDESS? Do you not Know that they Worship their Possessions, who are otherwise known in *Biblical Terms* as *BAAL Worshipers?* Indeed, that is what has made it Possible for them to make the Masses of People into their SLAVES, even as it is Written in Gold Lettering above the Courthouse Entrance in every City of Confusion on the Good Earth, saying: **Beware of the Slave Masters, who are Determined to make you and the Masses of Ignorant People into Education Slaves, Work Slaves, Tax Slaves, Insurance Slaves, Interest / Usury Slaves, Rent Slaves, Transportation Slaves, ElecTrickery Bills Slaves, Food Bills Slaves, Gas Bills Slaves, Water Bills Slaves, Repair Bills Slaves, Childcare Slaves, Entertainment Bills Slaves, and Endless BILLS SLAVES, while telling you and everyone else, over and over and OVER, that you are all FREE! Yes, you Live in the Greatest Nation on the Earth, they say, which is only 140 Trillion Dollars in DEBT to the Rich Edomites, which is True Freedom with a Capital T and F! But, be not Deceived by any Means: beCause Slavery is NOT True Freedom, nor is it Necessary that anyone should be a Slave of any Kind: beCause, if we just Sacrifice the False Ownership Doctrine on the Altar of Provable Truths, and Give Up that Silly Notion that we must OWN our own Private Swanky Palaces, we can all Work for only an Average of 4 Hours per Workday, and Eat at "Royal Swanky Buffets," and Live within "Beautiful Swanky PALACES" within those "GLORIOUS Swanky Hotels Castles and Fortresses!" Yes, we now have Mechanical Slaves that will be Happy to do most of the Difficult Work for us, and for FREE — that is, IF we all just Wake Up and CLAIM our own Mountains of Rocks, Minerals, Rivers, Lakes, Forests, and Sunrises, which the Great Creator God has Given to us Abundantly to Richly ENJOY — and all for FREE! †§‡§§**

02-07 [_] Well, my Friend, I Challenge you to get **those Words** Posted above any Courthouse Doors in the World, along with the following Inspired Words of Provable Truths: **A Righteous Government has an Unlimited Supply of New Money, which must be Earned by Honest Labor by "Seven Great Armies of Working Soldiers," who are Paid According to "A List of FAIR Swanky Wages," to Construct "Beautiful Planned City States for WISE Intelligent Well-Educated People with Common Sense and Good Understanding," which have more than 5,000 Advantages over Cities of Confusion: beCause they are "The Right Design for Living!" Yes, that Stonework will Represent that New Money, which will make it the very Best Money in all of the World, which must be Earned by Good Honest Labor, without any Loans, without any Interest, and without any Taxes, which must be Proven at: "The GREAT Worldwide TELEVISED Court HEARING!" (That Great Meeting of the Most Intelligent and Well-Educated Minds!) By The Worldwide People's Revolution!®**

02-08 [_] O Elected King, I have always Known within my Soul that there must be someone in this World of Wonders, who has **"Guaranteed Solutions!"** (HOW to Solve our Local and Global Problems in the Most Rational Manner Possible!) By **The Worldwide People's Revolution!®** Book 080. However, we are now up against a Great Tall THICK Solid Brick Wall of Unbelief: beCause the Masses of People are Brainwashed with Capitalist and Communist Lies!

02-09 [_] Well, my Friend, just be Patient: beCause, **"The Swanky Sword of Divine Truths"** has never Lost a single Battle in a Courtroom with a Righteous Judge in Charge of it!

02-10 [_] O Selected King, I Hope to God that *you* are that Riichus Juj.

— Chapter 03 —

Did any other Society ever Practice Swangkeenomiks?

03-01 [_] Well, not that I know of. However, it is Possible that the Atlanteans Practiced it — that is, IF they even Existed. Nevertheless, the Mayan Indians in Mexico had a somewhat Similar Swangkeenomiks System, whereby they all Worked Together as one large Family, and Shared their Tools, Toys, Possessions, Houses, Temples, and whatever: beCause they did not have Money. However, they had an Elite Class, who were Pampered, which is Contrary to my Master Plan, which Requires EVERYONE to do some Work, just to Grow some of their own Foods, in Order to Maintain Balanced Minds, and to Keep them in Contact with Nature and with Nature's God.

03-02 [_] So, O Selected King, suppose someone is simply not Successful with Growing their Fruit and Nut Trees, Berry Bushes and Vegetable Gardens, what shall be Done for them?

03-03 [_] Well, **the Swanky Association of Professional Gardeners** will Assist them, and Teach to them HOW to Do it Correctly: so that they are Successful. After all, it does not Require much Education to Plant a Fruit Tree, Correctly, nor to Gather the Fruits and Preserve them, Correctly; but, it does Require Cooperation with Nature, which Helps to Keep us Humble and Honest and Cooperative with Nature and with Nature's God in the Real World.

03-04 [_] So, O Selected King, do you Sincerely and Honestly Believe that you can Sell your Swangkeenomiks Plan to the Masses of People in this World of Woes? Will they not Rebel? After all, Swangkeenomiks Completely Destroys the American DREAM!

03-05 [_] Well, the "American Dream" is Actually the "American Nightmare," as I have said before: beCause it Produces X-amount of Criminals, which can be Proven in a Courtroom, just by Opening the Court Records. For Example, almost all of the *"Forty Eight Hours"* Programs on CBS TV are about Murders that were Committed by Greedy People, who Wanted someone's Money, which made Nightmares for them and whomever, including the Tax Slaves, who have to Cover the Costs of Maintaining Prisoners, Guards, Lawyers, Judges, Clerks, and so on, which the Mayan Indians did not have: beCause they did not have Money for People to be Lusting after. In other Words, they were much Wiser than the Normal White Chickens, who Crow about their False Riches, and Brag about their Abominable Toys. (Listen to C-SPAN, if you Doubt it.)

03-06 [_] O Selected King, I Want my own Personal Car, Motorboat, and Wooden / Plastic Firetrap Mouse-infested Cockroach Den, as you call those American Houses: beCause that is MY "American Dream," which is surely NOT a BAD Dream: beCause, even Jesus Christ and Moses Believed in Personal Possessions. (See *Claptrap 29:49, Edomite Banker's Version.*)

03-07 [_] Well, I will now Quote it directly from the *New Testament,* which you Pretend to Believe in. Therefore, please Check the Boxes with Statements that you Agree with:

> A-[_] And when the Day of Pentecost was fully come, the Self-disciplined Ones, who were True Followers of Jesus Christ, were all Gathered Together with one Accord in one Place

in a large Upper Room, Praying to God and Meditating on his Inspired Words of Provable Truths; and suddenly there came a Sound from the Sky, as of a Mighty Rushing Wind, and it Filled the entire House where they were Sitting, as if the entire House was Baptized by a Fire! Indeed, there Appeared unto them Flames of Fire, even as the Cloven Tongues of Fire that Leap from Burning Logs in a Fireplace, which Rested on each one of those Disciples, which Literally Baptized them with Fire, whereby they were Submersed in Fire; and thus their Spirits were Cleansed by Fire, and thus they were Filled with the Holy Spirit, and Immediately began to Speak with other Languages, even as the Holy Spirit gave to them Utterance, which Fulfilled that Saying of John the Baptist, who Clearly Stated that there would come a Holy One after him, who would Baptize with Fire, whom we know as Jesus Christ, to whom they were Praying.

B-[_] And at that Time there were Dwelling at Jerusalem certain Honest White Jews, even Devout Men of God from every Nation under the Sky, who had come there to Keep the Feast Days Holy: because they were True Believers, who were Gathered in that large Upper Room with the Disciples of Jesus Christ, who Witnessed what had Happened to those Disciples, who were not Burned by the Fire, in spite of being Baptized in it. Therefore, they ran into the Streets, and Announced with Loud Voices what had Happened in the Upper Room.

C-[_] Therefore, when that was Noised Abroad, a Multitude of People came Rushing Together, being Astonished by what they Heard from those Honest White Jews; but, when they Heard what those Disciples were saying, they were Greatly Confounded: because of the Fact that every Man Heard them Speak in his own Language! Therefore, they were all Amazed, and Greatly Marveled over it, saying one to another: "Behold, are not all of these Men, who Speak such Things, Galileans? Therefore, how is it that every Man can Hear them Speaking in own Languages, wherein we were Born among all of the Nations — even Parthians, Medes, Elamites, Ethiopians, Mesopotamians, and Men from all over Judea, Cappadocia, Pontus, and Asia, India, Japan, Phrygia, Pamphylia, in Egypt, and in the Parts of Libya about Cyrene, and Strangers of Rome, Greece, France, England, and Jewish Proselytes, Cretes and Arabians — we do Hear them Speak in our own Languages the Wonderful Works of the Gods; but, how is it Possible?" And thus they were Amazed, and were in Doubt about their own Sanity, saying to one another: "What does this Mean?" And others Mocked them, saying: "These Men are Obviously Full of New Wine; or, they have been Eating Magic Mushrooms."

D-[_] But, Peter Heard it, and Stood Up with the other 10 Disciples, and lifted up his Voice, saying: "You Men of Judea, and all of you who Dwell at Jerusalem, let the Truth of it be known to you, and Listen Carefully to my Inspired Words of Provable Truths: because these Men are NOT Drunken with Wine, nor have they been Eating Magic Mushrooms, nor Consuming any other Drugs, as some of you Falsely Suppose, seeing that it is only the third Hour of the Day, when no Man Drinks Wine, much less the Self-disciplined Ones of Yoshua Messiah, who have just finished Fasting for 40 Days and 40 Nights, whereby we have been Baptized with Fire, and Filled with the Holy Spirit, even as all of you can be: because this is that which was Spoken of by the Prophet Joel — *'And it shall come to pass during the Last Days, says the Hebrew God, that I will Pour Out of my Holy Spirit upon all Flesh; and thus your Sons and your Daughters shall Prophesy, and your Young Men shall See Visions of Things to Come, and your Old Men shall Dream Dreams of Things to Come; and on my True Servants, and on my Faithful Handmaids, I will Pour Out during those Days of my Holy Spirit, and they shall Prophesy Marvelous Things; and I will Show Great Wonders in the Sky above, and Send Signs on the Earth beneath, even Rivers Transformed into Blood, you might say, whereby the Water will not be Fit to Drink: beCause of the Poisons within the Water; and Great Factories will Produce Countless Horseless Wagons, which will Burn Ancient Fuels that come from the Ground, and thus their Wagons will Run by Fires, and Emit Vapors of Toxic Smoke, whereby the Sunlight will be Darkened, and the Moon will Appear like the Color of Faded Blood, before the Great and Notable Day of the Supreme Ruler will Come, when the Man with the Spirit of Elijah will Come, who will Restore the Truth to the People of the whole World, who will bring the Leaders of all Nations into Judgment, even as it is Written in the Books of Esdras, which Wise People will Study: because a New Righteous One-World Government must be Established before the Second Coming of Yoshua Messiah: because he will not Return for an Unholy Bride. Yes, his Church must be Purified, and Purged from all Sins, before the Anointed Savior can Establish his own Righteous One-World Government, which is made up of Holy Men, who have become Like him in all Ways, who have Purified themselves, even as he is Pure, by Means of much Fasting and Praying; and therefore, it shall come to pass, that whosoever shall Call on the Name of the Supreme Ruler shall be Saved from the Darkness of Ignorance, and whosoever Purifies himself, even as his Anointed Savior is Pure, shall be Saved for a Position within his Great Kingdom, which will be Established Over all of the Nations on this Earth.'*

E-[_] "O you Men of Israel, Hear these Words: Jesus of Nazareth, who was an Honest Man, who was Approved by God among you by Means of Miracles and Great Wonders and Marvelous Signs, which God did by him in the Midst of you, even as you yourselves Know for a Fact — him, being Delivered by the Determinate Counsel and Foreknowledge of the Gods, you have taken, and by Means of Wicked Hands have Crucified and Slain — whom the Hebrew God has Raised Up from the Dead, having Loosed him from the Pains of Death: because it was not Possible that he should be Held by the Angel of Death in the Grave: because he was Pure and Innocent, being the Chosen Son of God, who Selected him from among many Sons to be the Supreme Ruler of this World: because he was Found Worthy in another World of a Higher Order. Indeed, King David Spoke concerning him, saying: *'I Foresaw the Supreme Ruler in all of his Naked Glory in his Great Kingdom by Means of Marvelous Visions in front of my Face: because he Stands at my own Right Hand Side, so that I should not be Moved Away from my Faith in him. Therefore, my Heart Rejoices in him, and my Tongue is always Glad to Speak Well of him. Moreover, my Flesh shall also Rest in Hope: because he will not leave my Soul in the Grave, neither will he Allow his Holy One to see Corruption in his Grave. Indeed, you, O God, have made known to me the Ways of Life; and therefore, you shall make me Full of Joy by Means of your own Countenance in my Dreams.'*

F-[_] "Men and Brothers, let me Freely Speak to you about the Patriarch David, so that you might Know that he is both Dead and Buried, and his Sepulcher is with us until this very Day, which you may Visit in Person, even as the Graves of Abraham, Isaac, Jacob, and Joseph are in the Cave of Machpelah, which all of us Disciples have seen, which are Inscribed with their Names in Stones, which you may still read. Moreover, David has not

Ascended into Heaven, as some Foolish People still Vainly Imagine; but, he is still with us, until this very Day. ‡

G-[_] "Therefore, being a Holy Prophet, and Knowing that God had Sworn with an Oath to him, that of the Fruit of his own Loins, according to the Flesh, God would Raise Up Christ to Sit on his own Throne in the Great World Temple of Peace, in Jerusalem; David, seeing that in a Vision, Centuries Ago, Spoke of the Resurrection of Christ, that his Soul was not left in the Grave, nor did his Flesh see Corruption: because he was Healed and Resurrected. Yes, this same Jesus has God Raised Up, whereof we are all Witnesses, who saw him several Times after his Resurrection, in Person, after which he was Caught Up into the Sky by the Power of the Gods, and Disappeared among the Clouds in his Spacecraft, which we have also Seen many Times: because they are Common Objects in the Sky, which come Out from the Hollow Earth, even from the Holy City of the Great King, itself, which you can read about in *Psalms 48, 50, and 87*.

H-[_] "Therefore, being Exalted by the Right Hand of his Father God, and having Received of the Father the Promise of the Holy Spirit, he has Shed forth this Marvelous Thing that you have also now Witnessed, which you now See and Hear, and Know for a Fact that it is not any Trickery of Evil Men, nor any Deception of the Devil: because King David did not Ascend into the Heavens, nor are any of us going to Ascend into the Heavens when we Die: because this Earth is our Eternal Home, which we should Love and Care for, and make into a Good Place for everyone to Live and Work, by Means of United Effort, whereby we Love one another as much as we Love ourselves. Indeed, David himself said, *The Supreme Ruler said unto my Ruler, 'Sit yourself here at my Right Hand Side, until I make your Enemies like your Footstool, whom you shall Rule Over during the Last Days.'*

I-[_] "Therefore, let all of the Household of Israel Know Assuredly that God has made that same Jesus, whom you have Crucified, both the Ruler and the Anointed One."

J-[_] Now, when the Multitude Heard that, they were Pricked in their Hearts, and thus one of them Spoke for all of them to Peter and to the Remainder of the Apostles, saying: "Men and Brothers, what shall we Do?"

K-[_] Then Peter said to them, "Repent of all of your Sins, even as the Men, Women, and the Children of Nineveh Repented by Means of Fasting and Praying for 40 Days and 40 Consecutive Nights; and then be Baptized every one of you in Water, in the Name of Jesus Christ for the Remission of your Sins, whereby you too will Receive the Baptism of Fire, if God Finds you Worthy of it, and also the Gifts of the Holy Spirit, whereby you may also do Mighty Miracles, and even Greater Miracles than those that were Done by the Anointed Savior, himself: because of Receiving the Power of God: because the Promise is unto you, and to your Children, and to all who are afar off, even to as many People as might Believe, Love, and Obey his Commandments, who are Called by him for Positions within his Holy Kingdom, which is a Good Government, which will one Glad Day Govern the Whole Earth with Righteousness in Holiness." {See www.Amazon.com for: **"The Gospel According to our Elected King!" (The Good News from the Most Modern Perspective!) By The Worldwide People's Revolution!® Book 013.**}

L-[_] And with many other Words, Peter Testified and Exhorted the People, saying: "Save yourselves from this Corrupted Generation: because they are Doomed, if they do not Repent. Yes, they will be Cursed with Self-inflicted Punishments: because of Rejecting Truths without a Just Cause. Indeed, that is the Greatest of Sins: beCause it Causes all of the other Sins. Therefore, Think about it, Meditate on it, and do not Reject any Truth, even if it comes from the Mouth of Balaam's Ass: beCause God Uses the Weakest of People to bring about Great Things, in Order to Confound Worldly-wise People, who put their Trust in their much Learning, Ridiculous Philosophies, and Vain knowledge, who do not even Capitalize Faith, Hope, Trust, Love, Patience, Persistence, nor Obedience, which are **'The Seven Basic Spiritual Building Blocks of LIFE!'** In Fact, it will come to pass during the Last Days, before the Second Coming of Jesus Christ, that Wicked Men will Wax Worse and Worse: beCause of the many Lies of those Red Jews, who will Control the Money Supply, who will also Control the News, Book Publishing, Weapons Manufacturing, Chemical Corporations, Drug Companies, and the Government, itself, which will be called the Industrial Military Congressional Bankers' Complex: beCause those Rich Lying Red Jews will Control it. Yes, they will have their Sticky Fingers in everything that concerns Money: because they have their Hearts Set on the Vain Things of this World, rather than on the Glorious Things of the Gods."

M-[_] Then the Multitude Gladly Accepted his Inspired Words of Provable Truths, and were Baptized in Water unto Repentance, whereby there was Added unto them about 3,000 Souls that same Day, who Commenced to Fast and Pray for 40 Days and 40 Consecutive Nights; and thus they Continued Steadfastly in the Apostles' Doctrine and Fellowship with one another, until they were also Baptized with Fire and Filled with the Holy Spirit; and after that they Continued with them, in Breaking of Bread, Eating Sweet Fruits, and in Prayers: beCause they had Discovered the JOY of the Holy Ones. And thus Fear came upon every Soul who Saw their Holy Faces; and many Wonders and Great Signs were Done by the Apostles for Confirming Peter's Words, whereby many People Confessed their Sins, and were Baptized unto Repentance, and took up Fasting and Praying, whereby they were Saved from all of their Sins, and thus Stopped Sinning.

N-[_] And it came to pass that all who Sincerely Believed came Together on the Land that Fed and Clothed them, and had all Things in Common. Yes, they Sold all of their Possessions and Goods, and Distributed Food and Clothing to all People who were in Need, and also Bought Tools for themselves to Work with, whereby they might Build a Beautiful Planned City State for themselves, Outside of Jerusalem, where their Families might Live in Peace, and be Protected from the Wild Beasts. Moreover, the Apostles Continued to Meet Daily with One Accord in the Temple, and to Break Bread from House to House, whereby they Ate their Foods with Gladness and Singleness of Heart toward God: because they were not Attached to any Worldly Possessions, whereby they Rejoiced over the Fact that everyone had Plenty, and no Person Lacked for any Good Thing, for which they Praised God, and also had Favor with all of the People, who Loved them for their Generosity. And thus the Savior Added to the Church Daily such as should be Saved for Positions within his Good Government.

O-[_] Nevertheless, it came to pass that the Romans became Envious of them, and told them that they had to Cease Building the New City State, or else they would Slay them for it. Therefore, they left off Building it, and went about Preaching Repentance, with the Hope that most People would finally be Converted to the Truth, and would Eventually come to their Right Senses, and thus Build those Beautiful Planned City States, anyway.

P-[_] However, when the Red Jew Scribes and Pharisees Spied on them, and Discovered what they were up to, they Informed the Romans of it, and said that those Christians were Planning on taking Over the whole World, which Alarmed the Romans, who did not Want to Lose their Position of Power; and therefore, they began to Persecute them, and to Scatter them Out, which only Worked Against them: because those Christians took their Message to all of the Nations around there, which Infuriated the Romans as Time passed by, whereby they Persecuted them more and more, and even Crucified many of them, and Burned them while Tied to Trees, by Setting Forests on Fire with thousands of them Tied to Trees: because they were Power Hungry, Fearful, and Mean, being Possessed by Demon Spirits.

Q-[_] O Selected King, that is NO Quotation from the Holy Bible.

R-[_] So, the Great Question is: **"Which Boxes did you Check with an X?"** Indeed, which Statements do you Agree with? Are you Aware that God will Judge you According to your most Reasonable Responses to all such Statements? Indeed, during the Day of Judgment, all of the Books will be Opened Up, including this Inspired Book, and all of the Nations will be Judged by those Things that are Written in the Books.

S-[_] I Agree with that Statement; but, I am Afraid to Check the Box with an X: beCause, if I Check that Box, I will have to Check the other Boxes that I Agree with, whereby I will Prove myself to be WRong! Indeed, I already Checked the "Q" Box: beCause I Know for a Fact that it is not a Quotation from any Bible, which is WHY that I have also Checked the above Box for "S."

T-[_] It is Time for you to Stop and THINK, my Friend: beCause, if you have Checked the "Q" Box, you will be in Trouble during the Day of Judgment: beCause it is a Quotation from the New MAGNIFIED Version (NMV) of the *Scriptures,* which is God's Authorized Version, and the only Correct one: beCause it is Inspired by the Holy Spirit, whom you Dare not Blaspheme Against, lest you Commit the Unpardonable SIN!

U-[_] O Selected King, the Unpardonable Sin is the Greatest of Sins — NOT the Rejection of Truths, as Peter supposedly stated in Verse "L," above.

V-[_] Well, the only Reason that someone would Blaspheme the Holy Spirit, and Speak Evil of that which is Good, would be IF such a Person should Reject Truths without a Just Cause, including the Great Truths about SWANGKEENOMIKS!

W-[_] O Selected King, will we all go to Hell for Rejecting Swangkeenomiks? Is Swangkeenomiks the Financial Salvation of Mankind, or what?? Will we get ourselves into World War 3 on Account of Rejecting Swangkeenomiks?

X-[_] Well, X-amount of Ignorant People will just Naturally Reject Swangkeenomiks on Account of not Understanding the VIRTUES of it, while Ignoring the VICES and EVILS of CAPITALISM, which can be Proven in a Courtroom, even as I have already Proven in: **"The Nature of CAPITALISM!" (A List of the EVILS of CAPITALISM!)**, Book 038. Yes, the LOVE of MONEY is at the Heart of it, which is the Root Cause for almost all Evils, even as the Apostle Paul WARNED. {See www.Amazon.com for my Inspired Book, called: **"For the Love of Money!" (The Strange Things that People Say and Do to Get more Money!) By The Worldwide People's Revolution!®** Book 003.}

Y-[_] So, O Selected King, if we are Perfectly Honest with ourselves and with God, we will have to Confess that SWANGKEENOMIKS Rules the Roost, huh? Yes, Capitalism will be Hanged by its own Rope of Hopelessness: beCause Reason and Logic are on YOUR Side concerning this Important Issue: beCause there are more than 5,000 Good Reasons and Great Advantages for Building those Beautiful Planned City States, which no Righteous Person can Ignore, nor Honestly Deny: beCause the FACTS are on YOUR Side, O Selected King. Therefore, what was Good for the First Christians, during Yesteryears, is still Good for us, Today! Yes, True Christians will have to Confess that they Need to REPENT, even as Jesus said in *Matthew 12:40,* and take up Fasting and Praying, whereby they will Realize the NEED for a Beautiful Planned City State for True Christians, called: A New Jerusalem, which can be Built in the Great State of Flexible Texas, which has LOTS of Space for it. †§‡ {See: **"A New Jerusalem in the Great State of Flexible Texas!" (HOW to make Good Use of the Mississippi River!) By The Worldwide People's Revolution!®** Book 090.}

Z-[_] Well, I have to Agree with you — that there is Plenty of Space for it in Texas, which is mostly a "Wasteland," you might say — but, whether or not anyone will take up Fasting and Praying, until they are Baptized with FIRE, like the Apostles were, is another Subject: because the Federal Government will not Allow it: beCause such a Fortified City of Holy People would be a Great Threat to the EVIL Capitalist Empire: beCause they would not Need any of their Drugs, Cars, Trucks, Buses, Tractors, Lawnmowers, Weed-eaters, Motorboats, Motorcycles, Motor Scooters, and all of the EVIL Things that I have Listed in **"The Nature of CAPITALISM!" (A List of the EVILS of CAPITALISM!) By Master Mark Revolutionary Twain, Junior!** Book 038.

03-08 [_] O Selected King, are you Suggesting that there is something EVIL about Spraying RAAD up the Nostrils of the Baby Jesus? †§‡§§

03-09 [_] Well, would you Spray any Poisonous Abomination up the Nostrils of any Baby? If not, WHY would you Spray such Poisons into the Nostrils of yourself, your Children, and whomever might be in your House? Therefore, Try to Use your Brains to THINK before you ACT: beCause we shall all be brought into Judgment for our Words and DEEDS. ‡

03-10 [_] O Selected King, until Today, I had no Idea what it Means to: *"Come you Out from among the Wicked Ones, and be you SEPARATED from them, and Touch NONE of their Unclean Things, says the Most High God; and then I will Receive you, and will be a Loving Father unto you, and you shall become my Chosen Sons and Beloved Spiritual Daughters: because I will Adopt you into my Holy Family."* — NMV

— Chapter 04 —

Swangkeenomiks is Biblical!

04-01 [_] O Selected King, I could not Resist the Great "Temptation" to Read the New MAGNIFIED Version (NMV) of *First Timothy 6,* which can be found in: **"For the Love of Money!" (The Strange Things that People Say and Do to Get more Money!) By The Worldwide People's Revolution!®**, Book 003, which is one of the most Enlightening Pieces of Inspired Literature in all of the Whole World! In Fact, if I had Carefully Read that Chapter with a Capital R, when I was 12 Years of Age, my entire Life would have been Transformed, and perhaps Millions of People would have been Converted to the Truth. However, instead of the Prosperity Gospel Preachers Teaching those Great Truths, they Busy themselves with False Doctrines, and take up the Songs of the Drunkards with Broken Hearts: beCause of Transgressing one of the Basic Laws of God, whereby all Ministers of his Truths are Supposed to be Contented with FOODS and CLOTHING, just as the Apostle Paul told Timothy! Therefore, the Pope of Rome will be more Justified during the Day of Judgment than Oral and Richard Robbers and other Televangelists with that Prosperity Gospel Nonsense: because the Pope of Rome Lives a Modest Life, and Serves God without any Personal Lusts for any Vain Things. Indeed, he is Contented with his Comb and Toothbrush, you might say. †§‡

04-02 [_] Well, all such "Evangelists" just Naturally Seek the False Riches: beCause their Hearts are not Riit with God. Otherwise, they would be Contented with Foods and Clothing. However, you might have Noticed that Paul did not Mention HOUSING: beCause the Ministers' Houses were Provided by the Believers who Followed them, whereby the Ministers were not Encumbered by Burdensome Possessions — such as Houses and Lands to Attend to: beCause they Devoted their Full Attention to the Ministry, whereby they were much more Successful than their Modern "Counterparts," who have not *"... Turned the World Upside Down ..."* by any Means; but, they have Managed to Deceive X-amount of Ignorant FOOLS, who have been "Sowing Seed Money" in their Offering Plates, with the Hope of being "Blest with Father Abraham," who had much Silver and Gold, Servants and Livestocks.

04-03 [_] O Selected King, are you not Aware that "Livestock" is PLURAL, and not Singular? Indeed, I have Noticed that you WRongfully use the S on Sheeps, Bisons, Mooses, Feets, and many other Plural Words without any Justifications for it: beCause Ignorance is no Good Excuse for you. After all, you probably have more Learning than any of us. Therefore, you should Know that it is WRong to put an S on Sheeps and Livestocks. †§‡

04-04 [_] Well, if Sheep is Plural, what is a Singular Sheep? For Example, which one of you Sheep can Count 4 Bison Eating in the Pasture with Horse and Elephant, beyond those House, over yonder on the Mountains of Ararat, where Animal got out of the Ark, namely Goat, Hippopotamus, Turtle, Frog, Lizard, Snake and Skunk? However, Noah looked all around, and saw Cat, Mouse, Weasel, and Cow, and thus he said, "My Livestock know me by Name; but, neither Sheep nor Goat know me after talking with Dog and Cat, who gathered their Information from Moose and Elk, who are Prophet with long Hair, Beard, and Mustache, like Mose, who was the first British Monarch of Confusion, who was too Lazy to put an S on all Plural Word."

04-05 [_] O Elected King, are you Trying to Mock our Insane English Language, which has a hundred or more Dialect, Conjunction, Conjecture, Inflection, Semantic, Grammars, Cherubims, and Seraphims? What Crazy Schoolz of Ignorant Fools did you Attendz with Huck Finns and Nigger Jims? †§‡§§ {See www.Amazon.com for: **"The Public School of IGNERUNT FQLZ!" (HOW we have been GRAATLEE DISEEVD by Capitalism!), Book 024, plus: "Are you a Jobless Graduate of the SKQL uv FQLZ?" (HOW to get a GOUD EJUKAASHUN without Robbing the Bank!) By The Worldwide People's Revolution!® Book 020.**}

04-06 [_] Well, why not Follow Consistent RULES, just like the Spanish Language does, which puts an S or Z on Sheeps, Biisunz, Mqsuz, Liivstoks, Cheirubz, Seirufs, and so on? Yes, they Discovered "Funetik" Spanish several hundred Years Ago! However, it is not Totally Consistent: beCause it is also a Confounded Language with Contradictions. Nevertheless, it is much easier to Learn than English, which was likely Derived from Hebrew and Chinese, or perhaps from Aborigine and Swahili. After all, it was Satan who was in Charge of Confounding all of the Languages, which can be Proven in a Courtroom, who is still Causing much Unnecessary Confusion, Worldwide, even though the *Holy Bible* gives God the Credit for Confounding all of the Languages in *Genesis 11,* which is Contradicted by *First Corinthians 14:33, KJV.* †§‡

04-07 [_] O Selected King, I would Love to Read your NEW MAGNIFIED VERSION (NMV) of the Entire Bible: beCause it is Obviously far Superior to any other Version. Moreover, I Agree with you — that 2 Sheeps should be Distinguished from one Sheep by adding an S to it, whereby the Childrens will be less Confuse, and all of the Livestocks can get back into Noah's Arks: beCause he would have Needed no less than a THOUSAND Arks, just to Holdz all of the Waters for those Animal. †§‡§§

04-08 [_] O Selected King, your own Pen Name Means 2, as in Mark Twain. Therefore, are you 2 Peoples, or ones, being **The Worldwide People's Revolution!®**?? §

04-09 [_] Well, if a Bible has X-amount of Ignorance Deliberately Placed within it, in the Holy Name of some Imaginary Jewish God, who can Believe it to be "the Pure Words of God"? After all, if "God" made Sense, and only Spoke like a Person with a Rational Mind, half of the Bible would have to be TRASHED: beCause it makes little Sense, when it should make BIG Sense. Therefore, with such Insane Languages as English, Hebrew, and Swahili, is it any Wonder that "Christians" cannot Understand Muslims, who are at least Honest enough to Confess that the Qur`an is only Properly Understood in Arabic: beCause Arabic cannot be Properly Translated into English, nor can English be Properly Translated into Spanish: beCause the Spanish Language is MISSING many Important Words — such as "Right," "Trust," and "Love," as in Brotherly Love: beCause "Brotherly Love" Translates as having Brotherly SEX, and thus has no Connection with Brotherly Love, as English-speaking Peoples knowz it!

04-10 [_] So, O Selected King, what does any of that Nonsense have to do with whether or not the *Holy Bible* Supports SWANGKEENOMIKS?

(HOW all People can Prosper in a RIIT WAA, and Stop Polluting the Earth with Capitalist TRASH!)

— Chapter 05 —

Swangkeenomiks Rules the Roost!

05-01 [_] O Selected King, if that previous Person had Studied Verse 04-01, he or she would have Known whether or not the Bible Supports Swangkeenomiks — at least if one is a True Christian: beCause True Christians are not Attached to the Vain Things of this World, which are the Needless Things — such as those Stinking Noisy Polluting Automobiles, Lawnmowers, Chainsaws, Vacuum Cleaners, Hair Dryers, Electric Toothbrushes, Electric Razors, Toasters, Blenders, and all such Capitalist TRASH, which fills up Trash Dumps all around the World. However, that is not to say that True Christians are too Lazy to Build Beautiful Planned City States for themselves to Live within: beCause that is another Subject: beCause none of those Cities are VAIN Things. Indeed, People Need Good Comfortable Secure Houses to Live in, and Well-made Tools to Work with, and an Abundance of Wholesome Natural Foods to Eat, which can only be Obtained from the LAND, no matter HOW one goes about Getting those Foods. However, many People, nowadays, Vainly Imagine that Foods come from Grocery Stores and Restaurants, which they also Vainly Imagine are GOOD Foods: beCause, *"... it is not that which Enters into a Person's Mouth that Defiles him, ..."* they say, which is Partly True; but, it is taking the Truth, which Jesus Taught about it, OUT of Context with the Whole Truth that he Taught about it. {See www.Amazon.com for: **"Poverty Hunger Riots Strikes Brutalities Election Deceptions and Civil Wars!" (The High Price that we Earthlings have Paid for Leaving the Good Land!) By The Worldwide People's Revolution!® Book 014.**}

05-02 [_] Well, my Friend, you have probably Noticed that there are many Interpretations of the Teachings of Jesus: beCause his Words were either Mutilated, Deleted, Edited by Hypocrites, or just Mistranslated, as in *Acts 2*. Otherwise, there would not be more than 400 Different Major Religions with thousands of Contradictory Minor Sects among them. Indeed, the "Commonists" Believe somewhat like the Shakers of Shaker Villages during the 1800's, who *"had all things in common."* Yes, there is another Sect of "Commonists," who Translate that to Mean that they should also Share their Wives in Common with whomever Lusts after them: beCause, "ALL" Means ALL. However, that is a Mistranslation and a Mutilation of the Truths that the Bible Teaches about that Subject, which must be Accepted in CONTEXT with the Whole Book of Mutilated Books, which are Missing many Books. (See *Second Chronicles 9:29; and 12:15.*)

05-03 [_] So, O Selected King, were the Russian Communists Attempting to Love and Obey *the Book of Acts,* or what?? Were they Practicing Swangkeenomiks?

05-04 [_] NO, they were NOT Practicing Swangkeenomiks, which is Summed Up in the "Inset" following Verse 01-03, which no Government has ever Done, as far as I know, with the exception of the Government of King Solomon, which the Bible does not make Clear: beCause it was Obviously Mutilated by Lying Conniving Edomites, who Wanted to Control the Money Supply; and therefore, they Set Up BANKS for Loaning Money for USURY, or Interest, which Banks were never Needed: beCause People can Live Happily without them, even as a single Family can Manage its own Money, if a Righteous Father is in Charge of it, just by Learning, Believing, Loving, and Obeying *The New MAGNIFIED Version of the Ten Commandments,* which you can find in: **"LIGHTNING Verses the Lightning Bug!" (HOW almost Everyone can become Moderately RICH without Telling Any Lies nor Selling Any Trash!) By The Worldwide People's Revolution!®** Book 001. Indeed, if you were the Father of the Household, and you had 7,000,000 Children, and an Unlimited Amount of Money in your own Safe, you could Use that Money Wisely, in Order to HIRE your 7 Million Children to Build Swanky Stone Dome Homes for themselves within a Beautiful Planned City State, and the Stonework would Represent that New Money, which would make it GOOD Money: beCause it would have to be EARNED by Honest Labor, by your own Children. In other Words, being a Loving FATHERLY Government, instead of a Greedy Selfish BANKER, you could Use your Money WISELY, in Order to HIRE those **"Seven Great Armies of Working Soldiers"** to Build those City States, whereby they could Govern themselves, and Live in PEACE: beCause of Learning **HOW to Provide a Way for Everyone to WORK: so as to Eliminate Poverty, Crimes, Drug Abuses, Prisons and Unnecessary Taxes!** Yes, it is just that SIMPLE. Moreover, all of those Wise Children who Joined **"The Swanky Associations of Working Soldiers!" (A Fascinating Collection of Various Kinds of Voluntary Working Soldiers!)**, Book 018, would all become Moderately RICH: beCause of Building **"GLORIOUS Swanky Hotels Castles and Fortresses!" (Beautiful Planned City States for WISE Intelligent Well-Educated People with Common Sense and Good Understanding!)**, Book 019, which would contain **"Beautiful Swanky PALACES"**: beCause of Making **"The Environmentalists' Paradise!" (HOW almost Everyone could be Living in a Beautiful Manmade Paradise!)**, Book 035, which has no less than 5,000 Good Reasons and Great Advantages for Doing it! {See www.Amazon.com for: **"The Low Court of Supreme Injustices is Brought to Trial!" (Our Elected King Butts Heads with the United States Supreme Court, with or without their Black Robes of Hypocrisies and Lies!)**, Book 011, plus: **"The Right Design for Living!" (A List of Great Advantages for Building Beautiful Planned City States!) By The Worldwide People's Revolution!®** Book 012.}

05-05 [_] O Selected King, I must Confess that SWANGKEENOMIKS Rules the ROOST: beCause there is no other Potential King in this World, who can begin to Compete with you and your Master Plan for Worldwide Law, Order, Obedience, Peace, and True Prosperity! Yes, you are Truly the most Colorful Peacock who ever Lived, whose Squawk can be Heard for Miles in all Directions, and much Farther than any Rooster of any Color or Kind! †‡

05-06 [_] Well, if anyone in the World Imagines that he or she has a Better Master Plan than mine for Worldwide Law, Order, Obedience, Peace and True Prosperity, that Person should Present his or her Master Plan at: **"The GREAT Worldwide TELEVISED Court HEARING!"** Yes, it could be Possible; but, Highly Unlikely: beCause my Master Plan is a Revelation from GOD, which can be Proven in a Courtroom! Indeed, if you Doubt it, just Sit your Big Fat Ass down in front of your own Computer, and Invent a Better Tale of Wisdom and Truths than my own! †‡

05-07 [_] O Elected King, are you not Afraid of Offending other People with Fat Asses, which might only be Slightly Fatter than your own? †§‡

05-08 [_] Well, I do not have a Fat Ass, and never did have: beCause I "Lucked Out," as they say. Indeed, after Fasting for 314 Days during 14 Months, I could rest my Hand on my Belly, and Feel my own Backbone: beCause I Weighed about 100 Pounds, and I was 6 feet 3.5 inches Tall at the Time; or, about the same Height as President Abraham Lincoln, who Wore High-heeled Boots and a Stovepipe Hat, just to make himself Appear as a Giant of a Man, even though he was also a very

(HOW all People can Prosper in a RIIT WAA, and Stop Polluting the Earth with Capitalist TRASH!)

Skinny Person: beCause he did not have any Great Appetite to Compete with Lying Edomites, who often get their Just Rewards at their own Tables, who might be well Able to MOCK my Inspired Words of Provable Truths; but, it is for Certain that none of them could Invent anything so Beautiful as **"The Tale of the Peacock, and *The Rope of Hope,*"** which is a Marvelous Collection of more than 350 Inspired Books, which used to be Posted for Free on the Internet; but, then the Bankers' Great Recession came along, and we got Robbed of our 40-acre Farm (minus ½ acre), and thus Lost 30 Years of Hard Labor, and ALL of our Property, including 3 Stone Houses with Roofs 6-feet THICK, and Side Walls 17 feet thick at their Bases, which made them Fireproof, Tornado-resistant, somewhat Self-air-conditioned, and Paint-proof: beCause the Marble-faced Walls did not Need Painting, nor could the Houses ever Rot Down, as most American houses can. Indeed, I tell all about that Criminal Act by those Edomite Bankers, in other Books, who Robbed us of the Farm, after Investing more than 300,000$ in it, including our Father's Inheritance, and Collected a Total of 50,000$ when it was Sold, which amounted to less than 25 Cents per Hour for our Labors, and NOTHING for the Property, itself, which seemed to be GOOD to those Greedy Bankers, and also to the Real Estate Buyer, who never even put a Concrete Roof on the 100,000-gallon Cistern with 3-feet-thick Walls, which Required 7 Years of Hard Work, and most of it was my own. However, little did those Banksters know that God would get Revenge on them by Inspiring me to Reveal the Truth about them and their Military Industrial Congressional Bankers' Complex, whose Days are Numbered. Guaranteed! †‡ (See Book 074 in the rear end of this Book.)

05-09 [_] O Selected King, I would say that they Crossed the WRong Person, which will Prove to be a Fatal Mistake for them: beCause, by the Grace of God, I, and many other Wise People, are Fixing to SELL your Inspired Books for a Fair Profit, whereby we can put them OUT of Business! Indeed, I dare say that all Honest Hardworking People in the Whole World will take your Side concerning this Issue, and will Stand Up for you during the Day of Judgment, at: **"The GREAT Worldwide TELEVISED Court HEARING!" (That Great Meeting of the Most Intelligent and Well-Educated Minds!) By The Worldwide People's Revolution!®** Book 041.

05-10 [_] Well, I Thank you and all of them for that, and I Trust that you are Wise enough to Check all of the Boxes that you Agree with, within ALL of my Inspired Books: so that I might Justly Reward you with Positions within **"The New RIGHTEOUS One-World Government!" (HOW to Establish a Righteous One-World Government without Going to WAR!) By The Worldwide People's Revolution!®** Book 056.

— Chapter 06 —

Swangkeenomiks has NO Competition!

06-01 [_] O Selected King, we have never Heard of Swangkeenomiks, before now; and therefore, none of us have given any Thoughts to it. After all, who on the Earth could Imagine that his or her Standard of Living could be Raised by at least 10 Times, even if he or she were already RICH, and had lots of Money in the Bank? Indeed, Bill Computer Software Gates has Built a big Ugly Wooden / Plastic Mansion for himself, which a Fire could Destroy within an Hour or less; and therefore, his False Riches cannot Compete with True Riches, much less with **"GLORIOUS Swanky Hotels Castles and Fortresses!" (Beautiful Planned City States for WISE Intelligent Well-Educated People with Common Sense and Good Understanding!)**, Book 019, which will Cost TRILLIONS of Dollars, which only the New RIGHTEOUS One-World GovernMINT will have! {See www.Amazon.com for: **"The CONSTITUTION for the New RIGHTEOUS One-World GovernMINT!" (HOW all Peoples can get True Justice, and Celebrate the Great Year of JUBILEE!) By The Worldwide People's Revolution!®** Book 016.}

06-02 [_] Well, my Friend, I do Pity those so-called "Rich" People, who are Suffering with all Kinds of Ailments: beCause of Living on Inferior Foods, who have never even Tasted of a Delicious Fragrant Tree-ripened Mango of the Haden Variety, nor the Puree Variety, much less a really Good Cherimoya, which has been Grown by: **"The LUSCIOUS All-Mineral Organic Method of Gardening!" (HOW to Grow DELICIOUS Satisfying Foods for Potential Kingz and Kweenz in Swanky PALACES!)**, Book 021: beCause their Standard of Living is Actually very LOW, when Compared with what it could be, should be, and will be within **"The Environmentalists' Paradise!" (HOW almost Everyone could be Living in a Beautiful Manmade Paradise!) By The Worldwide People's Revolution!®** Book 035.

06-03 [_] O Selected King, it Reminds me of *Revelation 3—4*:

> A-[_] And unto the Angel of the Church in Sardis, write: These Things says he who has the Seven Spirits of the Great Gods, and the Seven Great Stars are in his Right Hand — I know your Works, O Dietary Sinners, and I Confess that you do have a Name and Reputation that you Live; but, behold, you are Spiritually Dead in Trespasses and Sins.

> B-[_] Be Watchful, therefore, and Strengthen the Good Things that Remain about you, who are Ready to be Destroyed, and are about to Die: because I have not found your Works to be Perfect in front of your Hebrew God.

> C-[_] Therefore, Remember how you have Received the Truth, and have Heard the Good News; and thus Hold Tightly to all that is Good, and Repent of all of your Sins. However, if you shall not Watch, and be Ready for my Coming, I will Come on you like a Thief, and you shall not know what Hour that I will Come upon you.

> D-[_] Indeed, you have a few Names of Holy Men in Sardis, who have not Defiled their Garments with Painted Skunks; and they shall Walk with me in White Robes: because they are found Worthy; but, most of you are Defiled with Drugs, and Poisoned with Lies.

> E-[_] He who Overcomes all of his Sins, and Stops Sinning, the same Person shall be Clothed in White Robes; and I will not Blot Out his Name from the Book of Life, nor hold him in Contempt; but, I will Confess his Name in front of my Heavenly Father, and in front of his Holy Angels.

> F-[_] Therefore, he who has Spiritual Ears that can Hear, let him Hear what the Holy Spirit says unto the Churches.

> G-[_] And to the Angel of the Church in Philadelphia, write: These Things says he who is Holy, he who is True to his Words, he who has the Key of David, he who Opens, and no

(HOW all People can Prosper in a RIIT WAA, and Stop Polluting the Earth with Capitalist TRASH!)

Man can Shut; and Shuts, and no Man Opens — I know your Works, also, and you have done much Evil in my Name. Behold, I have set in front of you an Open Door of Great Opportunities, and no Man can Shut it by any Means: because some of you have a little Strength, and have Kept my Words in your Hearts, and have Obeyed my Commandments and have not Denied my Name, which Means the Anointed Savior in Plain English.

H-[_] Behold, I will make them who are of the Synagogue of Satan, who say that they are Jews; but, they are not True Israelites by any Means: because they tell Lies, and Greatly Exaggerate their Stories; behold, I will make them to come and Worship in front of your Feets, and to Know for a Fact that I have Loved you, O Israelites: because you Love and Obey my Commandments, and do not do Evil Works: because you Live Righteous Lives.

I-[_] Therefore, because you have been Patient, and Kept my Words in your Hearts, I will also Keep you from the Hour of Temptations, and from the Great Tribulation, which will come upon all of the World, in Order to Test the Spirits of all People who Live on the Earth.

J-[_] Behold, I will Come Quickly to my Great Temple, if you Establish a New Righteous One-World Government, and Do what is Right for one another. Therefore, Hold Tightly to that which you have Established in my Name: so that no Man should take Away your Crown.

K-[_] He who Overcomes all of his Sins, and Stops Sinning, him will I make like a Pillar in the Temple of my God, and he shall no longer go Out; and I will Write upon him the Name of my God, and the Name of the City of my God, which is a New Jerusalem, which will come down from Heaven, from my God; and I will Write upon him my New Name: because he is Worthy.

L-[_] He who has Spiritual Ears that can Hear, let him Hear what the Holy Spirit has to Say to the Churches.

M-[_] And unto the Angel of the Church of the Laodiceans, write: These Things says the Finalizer, the Faithful and True Witness, even he who was the Beginning of the Creation of God in this World of Wonders, who is called Adam, who was the First White Man, who brought about the Fall of Mankind by Eating the Forbidden Fruit, which Symbolized all Forbidden Foods; but, Especially Forbidden Knowledge, which cannot Satisfy the Soul: because only True Nolij can Satisfy the Soul. Nevertheless, I know your Works, that you are neither Hot nor Cold: because you have been Greatly Deceived by your Adversary, the Devil. However, I would have you to be either Hot or Cold.

N-[_] So then, because you are Lukewarm, and neither Hot nor Cold, I will Spit you Out of my Mouth, you might say: because you do not Taste Good to me: because you say, "I am Rich, and Increased with many Goods, and have Need of NOTHING; but, you do not know that you are Wretched, Miserable, Poor, Blind, and even Naked: because of your Great Pride and Drunkenness! Yes, you are Greatly Deprived of the Best Things in Life, while getting up every Morning like a Proud Rooster, who Crows about your Goodness and Greatness — even the Splendor of your Abominations, which I Hate.

O-[_] Therefore, I Counsel you to Buy from me Gold that has been Tested in the Fiery Furnace: so that you might be Rich with the True Riches; and Buy White Robes of Righteousness, so that you might be Clothed with Purity, so that the Shame of your Nakedness does not Appear; and Anoint your Eyes with Eye Salve, so that you might See everything Clearly.

P-[_] Remember this, as many People as I Love, I Rebuke and Chasten them for their Sins. Therefore, be Zealous and Repent: beCause it is the only Way that you can be Saved for any Position within my Holy Kingdom, if you become Holy, even as I am Holy.

Q-[_] Behold, I Stand at the Doorway of your House of Love, and Knock. Therefore, if any Man shall Hear my Voice, and Open the Door of his Heart, I will Come into him, and will Feast with him at the Table of Satisfaction, and he with me: because only the Sweet Fruits of Provable Truths can Satisfy the Soul.

R-[_] Therefore, to him who Overcomes all of his Sins, and Stops Sinning, will I Grant to Sit with me on my Golden Throne, even as I also Overcame the Devil in the Wilderness of Temptations by Fasting and Praying, and am now Sat Down with my Heavenly Father on his Golden Throne, which is Decorated with Gemstones of Various Kinds, which Symbolize the Gems of Truths and Wisdom.

S-[_] He who has Spiritual Ears that can Hear, let him Hear what the Holy Spirit says to the Churches.

T-[_] After that, I Looked into the Sky; and behold, a Door was Opened in the Sky; and the First Voice, which I had Heard, was as it were the Voice of a Trumpet Speaking with me: because it was so Loud, which said: "Come Up here, and I will Show to you Strange Things that must be hereafter."

U-[_] And Immediately I was Out of my Body, being Carried Away into the Sky by the Spirit of God, who has all Power Over Spirits; and, behold, a Throne was Set Up in the Sky, and a Holy One sat on the Throne, whose Flesh was like the Color of Jasper and Carnelian Stones, being Reddish Brown, and Glowing in the Light; and there was a Rainbow of Colors around the Throne, like Polished Emeralds, Sapphires, Rubies, and Precious Gemstones; and round about the Throne were 24 Seats for the 24 Elders, including the 12 Sons of Jacob, who were the 12 Disciples of Christ, including the Apostle Paul, who was Joseph Reincarnated, being Clothed with White Robes with Blue and Green Trimmings; and the other 12 Elders were Enoch, Melchizedek, Abraham, Isaac, Jacob, Moses, Joshua, Gideon, Elijah, Samuel, David and Jonathan; and they had on their Heads Crowns of Gold with Various Gemstones in the Crowns, which Symbolized the Great Truths that they had Learned.

V-[_] And out of the Throne proceeded Lightnings and Thunderings and Voices that I could not Understand; and there were Seven Lamps of Fire Burning in front of the Throne, which Symbolize the Seven Spirits of the Great Gods. And in front of the Throne there was a Sea of Glass, like Pure Crystal; and in the Midst of the Throne, and round about the Throne, there were 4 Strange Beasts full of Eyes, in front and behind: so that they could See in all Directions, which Symbolized the Great Kingdoms of the World.

(HOW all People can Prosper in a RIIT WAA, and Stop Polluting the Earth with Capitalist TRASH!)

W-[_] The First Beast was like a Lion, which Symbolized Babylon; the Second Beast was like a Calf, which Symbolized Greece; the Third Beast had the Face of a Man, which Symbolizes the Roman Empire; and the Fourth Beast was like a Flying Eagle, which Represented the Last Great Kingdom of Men on the Earth, which will Fly like an Eagle. Indeed, each of the 4 Beasts had 6 Wings about him, which had Eyes within them; and they do not Rest, neither Day nor Night; but, every Hour they Chant the same Song, saying: "Holy, Holy, Holy, Supreme Ruling God Almighty, which was, and is, and is to Come," which was Speaking of Jesus Christ, who was Adam, who was the Redeemer, and who is the Savior to Come, who will Reign as KING of Kings and RULER of Rulers Over all of the Nations.

X-[_] And when those Beasts gave Glory and Honor and Thanks to him who Sat on the Throne — who Lives forever and ever, who has been made Immortal, even like his Heavenly Father — the 24 Elders fell Down in front of him who Sat on the Throne, and Worshiped him who Lives forever and ever, and thus Cast their Crowns in front of the Throne, saying:

Y-[_] "You are Worthy, O Ruler, to Receive Glory and Honor and Power: because God has Created all Things in this Heaven and Earth just for you, according to your Desires, and for your Pleasure they are and were Created. Therefore, Thank you for Sharing all of these Marvelous Things with all of us."

Z-[_] And thus the Lightnings and Thunderbolts Spoke with a Hearty, AMEN.

06-04 [_] That is really Weird, O Selected King! Are you Sure that anything like that ever Happened?

06-05 [_] Well, it was just a VISION of Things to Come. Can you Deny that the Symbol for the United States of America is an EAGLE? Just Look at the Presidential Seal. Look at the Great Seal of the United States in *Wikipedia*. Notice that everything is Symbolical about it, and there are dozens of Interpretations.

06-06 [_] So, O Selected King, is your Sign and Seal for the New Righteous One-World Government easily Interpreted in a dozen or more Ways? {See www.Amazon.com for: **"God Speaks and the Whole World Listens!" (Fire on the Mountain from the Burning Bush by the Spirit of Truth!)**, Book 026, plus: **"FREEDOM uv SPEECH!" (U Speshoul Maguzeen uv Onist Upinyunz!) By The Worldwide People's Revolution!® Book 030-0001.**}

06-07 [_] Well, my Sign and Seal has only ONE Interpretation, which is my own, which you can find Explained in the above Book 026.

06-08 [_] So, O Selected King, how come our Forefathers did not Think of Establishing a New RIGHTEOUS One-World GovernMINT?

06-09 [_] Well, in their Viewpoint, they were doing very Well to Win the Revolutionary War against the Greatest Empire in the World, without Waging War against the whole World: because WAR was the one and only "Solution" for Obtaining Power during those Days; but, now we can

Exercise the Sword of Truths, and avoid any Hateful Wars. After all, the Good Things that I Propose are Acceptable by all Intelligent Well-Educated People, Worldwide. Indeed, I have NO Opposition Party to Contend with: beCause no one in the World Challenges my Master Plan for Worldwide Law, Order, Obedience, Peace, and True Prosperity. Therefore, I am already the KING of the New Righteous One-World GovernMint, even without an Election: beCause I have no Challengers! Moreover, no one has Presented any Reasonable Argument against Swangkeenomiks: beCause it Guarantees every Working Person in the World a Good Income, and a Swanky Palace, if they Want to Live in one. ‡ {See: **"All of the Arguments are in Favor of our Selected King, who has Zero Challengers!" (Before you Attend another Election Deception, you should Carefully Study this Inspired Book with an Honest Open Mind!) By The Worldwide People's Revolution!® Book 085.**}

06-10 [_] O Selected King, if your Plan were Workable, we would have already been Following it. Surely you are not the First Person to ever Think of Swangkeenomiks, which is Basically a Master / Servant Economic System, whereby X-amount of Masters Rule Over X-amount of Voluntary Servants, and all of them Work for an Average of only 4 Hours per Day, 6 Days per Week, or the Equivalent thereof, for 6 Years of Labor, and then they Retire in their Swanky Palaces, Debt-free, Rent-free, Tax-free, Insurance-free, and without any Bills to Pay. Therefore, who could Turn Down such a Good Deal as that? Moreover, if we Want to OWN our own Multi-million-dollar Swanky Stone Dome Home Complexes, we are Welcome to do that, also, if we can Earn enough Money to Pay for them. But, why bother? Why not just Accept our Fate when we Die, and to Hell with any Inheritances? Indeed, the Children can also be Happy to Live in those Swanky Palaces, and do their 4 Hours of Common Labor per Day, or the Equivalent thereof, and be Thankful that they do not have to Live in a Rusty Old Used Van down by the Polluted River, nor Sleep in some Subway or Sewage System with "Huck Finn and Nigger Jim."

— Chapter 07 —

Will Swangkeenomiks Eliminate Homelessness?

07-01 [_] Do you know of anyone in the whole World, who is too Lazy, or Unwilling to Trade 4 Hours of Common Skilled Labor per Day for the Privilege of Living in a King's Palace, having his or her own Private Stone Dome Home Complex with a Spacious Living Room 24—40 feet Wide, a Kitchen / Dining Room that is 20 to 24 feet Wide, which is Connected by a Tunnel to a Walk-in Cooler / Freezer / Pantry / Storage Dome, which is Connected to a Luscious All-Mineral Organic Garden, Vineyard, and Orchard? Frankly, I would say that if anyone is not Willing to Trade 4 Hours of Common Skilled Labor to get to Live in such a Stone Dome Home Complex with no less than 3 Spacious Bedrooms and Bathrooms, a Game Room for a Pool Table, or whatever, and a Home-craft Workshop with Well-made Tools to Work with, such a Person Deserves to Live in some Stinking little Apartment, with barely enough Space to turn around, and also have to take a Shower in a Stall that is 2 feet by 2 feet with the Bathroom Toilet between his Legs while Living in some Stinking Noisy City of Confusion with Terrorists Lurking all about.

07-02 [_] So, O Elected King of **The Worldwide People's Revolution!®**, the Major Problem during the Future will be Communicating this Message to those Ignorant Homeless People, huh?

07-03 [_] Well, Missionaries can go Talk with them, and Show to them many Pictures, if they cannot Read, whereby they might Learn about those **"GLORIOUS Swanky Hotels Castles and Fortresses!" (Beautiful Planned City States for WISE Intelligent Well-Educated People with Common Sense and Good Understanding!) By The Worldwide People's Revolution!®** Book 019.

07-04 [_] So, O Selected King, it is just a Matter of Time, and almost everyone in the World will Learn about those Beautiful Planned City States, huh?

07-05 [_] Well, we will only have to Build ONE of them for a Good Example, whereby the Gossip about them would Spread like Wildfire — that is, IF we do a Good Job of it, as if doing it for God, himself. (See *Deuteronomy 6:5*.)

07-06 [_] So, O Selected King, would the Capitalist Pigs not Envy us for it, even as the Romans Envied the First Christian Church, and thus Ordered them to STOP Building their New City, even as you have Revealed in Chapter 03-07?

07-07 [_] Well, there is a Cure for that Problem, if Enough People Cooperate: beCause it is Possible to put all of those Capitalists Hogs OUT of Business, by simply not Shopping for anymore of their Trash! And then we will have more Money to Buy and Sell more Copies of my Inspired Books, until the World is Flooded with them, until the Masses of Homeless People, Worldwide, will at last DEMAND **"The GREAT Worldwide TELEVISED Court HEARING!"** Yes, that will be the END of Confusion or Babylon. (See Book 050.)

07-08 [_] So, O Selected King, what are the Chances of Persuading even ONE Person to Believe in Swangkeenomiks, if Homeless Beggars cannot bring themselves around to Confessing that it would be much Better for them to be Living within **"Beautiful Swanky PALACES,"** than to be Living in Sewage Systems and Subways under Cities of Confusion, or Sleeping in their Cars, or under Bridges, and in Culverts: beCause of not having Houses to Live in? Indeed, as soon as they Hear that they might have to do 4 Hours of Work per Day, for 6 whole Years, building their own Swanky Stone Dome Home Complexes, Swimming Pools, Gymnasiums, Tennis Courts, Theaters, Game Rooms, Workshops, and Sales Shops, they seem to Lose all Interest in the Idea: because most People Want the Bankers to OWN their own Houses, even if they are Wooden / Plastic Firetrap Mouse-infested Cockroach Dens: beCause then they can BRAG about Owning their own Houses, which Actually Belong to those Rich BANKERS. However, they tell themselves that THEY are the Proud Owners of them, when they are Actually just Interest Slaves, Insurance Slaves, Tax Slaves, and Work Slaves, who now have to Work for 16 Hours per Day, just to SURVIVE! Yes, much of their Money is Wasted on Transportation: beCause they have not yet Discovered the Convenience and SPEED of Electric Elevators and Subway Trains at Swanky Fortresses, which are Designed for LIVING! †§‡ {See www.Amazon.com for: **"The Right Design for Living!" (A List of Great Advantages for Building Beautiful Planned City States!)**, Book 012, plus: **"Poverty Hunger Riots Strikes Brutalities Election Deceptions and Civil Wars!" (The High Price that we Earthlings have Paid for Leaving the Good Land!)**, Book

014, plus: **"Seven Great Armies of Working Soldiers!"** (HOW to Provide a Way for Everyone to WORK: so as to Eliminate Poverty, Crimes, Drug Abuses, Prisons and Unnecessary Taxes!), Book 015, plus: **"Does a Good Soldier have to be a MURDERER?"** (Seven Great Swanky Armies of Voluntary Working Soldiers!) By The Worldwide People's Revolution!® Book 027.}

07-09 [_] Well, when Ignorant People Believe LIES — such as Owning their own Houses and Vehicles, which Actually Belong to Bankers — then they Live in what is called a "DELUSION," or a FANTASY, whereby they Sincerely Believe an Outlandish LIE, which is only Discovered after a Great Recession, or a Great Depression, at which Time they end up being Homeless! However, not even Homeless People are Willing to Confess the Whole Truth about any Number of Important Subjects: beCause of Living in that Delusion. Indeed, they still Sincerely Believe that those Rich Bankers are the GOOD Guys, and that the Federal Government can do no WRong! Yes, they have lots of Faith in LIES — such as Men Landing on the Moon, when there is Zero Proof of it. (See Chapter 01-04-R.) Moreover, if something Really BAD does not Happen to them: beCause of Government Lies — such as Contracting Cancer from being Exposed to the Clouds of Asbestos in New Yuck City during September 11—November, 2001 — they are Unlikely to come to their Right Senses, and Confess that their Anti-Christ FALSE Cover-up Government is Actually SATANIC! Indeed, they should Study Howard Zinn's book, called: **"A People's History of the United States,"** which Lists dozens of EVILS that were Committed by the Federal Government, beginning with Saint Columbus Murdering some 20,000 Arawak Indians!

07-10 [_] O Selected King, you are only Looking at the NEGATIVE Side of the American Coin, instead of the POSITIVE Side. Indeed, there is not a Better Nation of People on the whole Earth! In Fact, our 2 Million-plus Prisoners get lots of Macaroni and Imitation Cheese to Eat, which is much Better than Whole Corn Tortillas in Mexico with Refried Beans and Chili Peppers, which just pass on through the Bowels, and does not even make those Prisoners FAT. Moreover, Americans get to use Drugs: because they are Rich, while those Poor Mexicans cannot even Afford Drugs. Therefore, you must Learn to Look at the POSITIVE Side of Living, and get your Mind OFF from all of those Negative Things. †§‡§§

— Chapter 08 —

Will Swangkeenomiks Provide Free Health Care Insurance?

08-01 [_] Well, one of the Greatest Advantages for Building Beautiful Swanky Fortresses is the Fact that People will be Assisted in a Right Way to become HEALTHY, Wealthy, and WISE, whereby they will not Need Health Care Insurance: beCause they will be Truly Healthy, even as we will Prove at **"The GREAT Worldwide TELEVISED Court HEARING!"** Yes, the Wise People of the World will Explain all such Things to us, and the Healthiest People will be Discovered, along with HOW they Obtained and Maintained Good Health. However, just to make

(HOW all People can Prosper in a RIIT WAA, and Stop Polluting the Earth with Capitalist TRASH!)

Sure that everyone is Cared for, and Properly so, **"The New RIGHTEOUS One-World Government"** will be the one and only "Insurance Company." Therefore, there will be nothing to Worry about, if we Establish a New Righteous One-World Government, and put Righteous People in Charge of it, who can be Discovered by Studying the SURVEYS of their VALUES. †‡ {See: **"The Complete SURVEYS of our VALUES!" (SURVEYS of Religious Spiritual Political Governmental Sexual Social Moral Economic Business Labor Habitual and Miscellaneous VALUES!) By The Worldwide People's Revolution!®** Book 059.}

08-02 [_] So, O Selected King, do you Sincerely Believe that any such Government could be TRUSTED to Provide GOOD Health Care? Will that Government not Favor the Rich People, and Deprive the Poor People of those Life-giving DRUGS? †§‡

08-03 [_] Well, in the System that I Propose, everyone will become Moderately Rich; and therefore, there will be no Excessively Rich People, nor any Extremely Poor People, Worldwide. Therefore, the New Righteous One-World Government will be Favoring EVERYONE who is Willing to Learn and Work, and without many College Degrees: beCause only a few People Need any such Degrees, and they will not be Paid any more than Common Working Soldiers: beCause they will have Lighter, easier Work to do. ‡

08-04 [_] So, O Selected King, if someone Diligently Studies the Stars, and Discovers something Special going on out there, will such a Person not be Rewarded for his or her Diligence?

08-05 [_] Well, if they Discover how to Prevent Cancers by Studying the Stars, I suppose that we could Reward such a Person with a Diamond-studded Dunce Cap, like College Graduates wear at their Graduate Ceremonies, whereby everyone might Know that they are Worthy of it. But, it does Sound a little Ridiculous to me. § {See www.Amazon.com for: **"Did God or Satan Ordain Medical Doctors??" (Ask Huck Finn and/or Nigger Jim: because neither Tom Sawyer nor Judge Thatcher would Know!) By The Worldwide People's Revolution!®** Book 022.}

08-06 [_] O Selected King, will we not even Need Medical Doctors with Swangkeenomiks?

08-07 [_] Well, once it is Proven that they are not Needed, we will only have to Love and Obey Natural Dietary Laws. †‡ {See the above Link for: **"DIETS!" (A Reasonable Solution for the "Eternal Controversy"!) By The Worldwide People's Revolution!®** Book 037.}

08-08 [_] O Selected King, are you saying that our Good Health Depends on our DIETS? I have been of the Persuasion that it is not that which Enters into our Mouths that Defiles us; but, it is only that which comes Out of our Mouths — such as Cursing, Filthy Jokes, and Evil Thoughts.

08-09 [_] Well, if we have Evil Thoughts, we will just Naturally have Evil Appetites, which will Cause us to Eat and Drink those Things that are no Good for us, or even Smoke Weeds and Chew on Tobacco, which are Addictive, whereby we can make Fools of ourselves, while Imagining that we can Eat anything that is found for Sale, including Drugs. However, Holy People have no Need nor Desire for any of those EVIL Things, which never did Profit anyone anything; but, those Evil Things did DECEIVE many People, including General George Washington, who did not Live out half of his Days, when he could have Lived for 120 Years in Good Health, after Establishing a RIGHTEOUS GovernMint, whereby almost everyone could have become Moderately Rich in

America, rather than make Interest Slaves of themselves to Rich Greedy Bankers, and Tax Slaves of themselves to Selfish Politicians and Warmongers. ‡

08-10 [_] O Selected King, I have no Faith in your Health Care Plan, even though I Know that you have not been to a Medical Doctor in more than 50 Years, and have not used any Medicines nor Drugs during all of that Time: beCause I am not as Self-disciplined as you are. Indeed, I Yield to the Temptations of the Devil: beCause I cannot Resist those Dainty Foods that are found for Sale. In Fact, I cannot even pass on by a Hamburger Shop without getting one to Eat. Therefore, I Need some Health Care Insurance to Cover my Lusts and Indulgences. †§‡

08-11 [_] Well, if you Want to Waste your Money on it, you are Welcome to do so; but, I will simply Trust the Righteous Natural Doctor Good Health to Care for me.

08-12 [_] O Selected King, what would you do, if you got run over by a Bicyclist at a Swanky Fortress, which Broke your Collar Bone? Would you go to a Doctor, or not?

08-13 [_] Well, no Bicycle Paths will be Pedestrian Paths at Swanky Fortresses. Therefore, that is unlikely to Happen. Nevertheless, if it did Happen, I would not Object to going to a Naturopathy Doctor. After all, each Swanky Fortress will have at least one of those Good Doctors, who will also be a Chiropractor. Moreover, there might even be a Doctor Knife hanging around, just in case some Child falls down with a Spoon in his Mouth, and Wounds himself.

08-14 [_] No Educated Parent would Allow such a Thing to Happen, O Selected King.

08-15 [_] Well, just about anything can Happen, unexpectedly. Therefore, it is Best to have Hospitals and Doctors at all Swanky Fortresses, even if they are not Needed; and most of them would never be Needed, which Means that they could do their Gardening, and Attend to their Studies of Healthy People. After all, there must be something more to Good Health than just Good Luck.

— Chapter 09 —

Swangkeenomiks Requires Money and LOTS of it!

09-01 [_] There are some People who say that our Economy does not Need any Money at all; and that all Money should be done Away with, as if People might just Voluntarily Work for NOTHING, and for the Benefit of the Community! Well, if they were True Christians, they might do that. However, when a Community has nothing to Contribute to the Community, how can the Community Prosper? Indeed, that Community would Need some LAND to Build their Houses on, which they do not have: beCause they have Forsaken the Land, and have now Crammed themselves up like Sardines in Tin Cans, with nothing to Work with. †§‡

(HOW all People can Prosper in a RIIT WAA, and Stop Polluting the Earth with Capitalist TRASH!)

09-02 [_] O Selected King, it Requires much more than just Land, in Order to Prosper in a Right Way. Indeed, it Requires Building Materials, Tools, and Skilled Craftsmen, which Requires Education, which Requires Schools and Teachers and Books, which Require MONEY: beCause we cannot have all of those Good Things without LOTS of Money.

09-03 [_] Well, that is also my Belief — that it Requires LOTS of Money, and a thousand Times as much Money as most People Realize — that is, IF anyone is Interested in Living in a Manmade PARADISE, which is the Ideal Way to Live, whereby everyone is Moderately RICH, just by Means of their Labors, alone, which Requires a New RIGHTEOUS One-World GovernMINT, which has an Unlimited Supply of Good Money, which must be Earned by Honest Labor: beCause that is the ONE and ONLY Way that anyone can Get it, without any Loans, without any Interest, without any Taxes, and without any Police DEPARTments, Lawyers, Criminal Judges, Jails, Prisons, Guards, Medical Doctors, Red Jew Propagandist Liars, nor Politicians: beCause Adam and Eve Lived Happily without them, and so can we. Moreover, Jesus Christ and his Disciples also Lived Happily without those Things, and so can we. Indeed, we who Believe that will have to SEPARATE ourselves from the Ignorant Idiots, just to be Able to Do that; but, it is most Practical to do so. †

09-04 [_] O Master Twain, it is my Belief that if all True Christians SEPARATE themselves from the Unbelievers, and Build just ONE of those **"GLORIOUS Swanky Hotels Castles and Fortresses!" (Beautiful Planned City States for WISE Intelligent Well-Educated People with Common Sense and Good Understanding!)**, Book 019, the other People will Sit Up and take Notice of it, and soon Want to Do Likewise! Yes, they will Discover that those True Christians are Truly RICH with the True Riches, being Healthy, Wealthy, and WISE. Therefore, they will soon Join Forces with them, and go to Work on the Construction of their own Beautiful Planned City States — except that none of them will have Sufficient MONEY for Doing any such Work: beCause there is NO Righteous One-World GovernMINT. Moreover, if they Printed up their own New Money, no one on the "Outside" would Accept it as True Money: beCause it would not be Accepted as "Legal Tender." Indeed, it would not be "Authorized" by the Federal Government of **"The Divided States of United Lies!" (The so-called "United States of North America" in Disguise!)**, Book 058, which would Naturally be Looking for Ways to TAX all such People, which is WHY it is Unconstitutional to Build a City State within a State.

09-05 [_] Well, what you are Proposing would be Good for those "Believers," of whatever Religion; but, then there would be a million Different Kinds of Phony Money in this World, if each Planned City State did the same Thing, and Printed its own Money, which would only bring in more Massive Confusion, Counterfeiting, Bribing, Stealing, Swindling, Wasting Time Exchanging Money, and whatever: beCause X-amount of People in the World would just Naturally be ENVYING the Righteous People, and they would be Trying to take Advantage of them. For Example, what Money would those Christians Use for Buying a Mountain of Rocks to Work with, in Order to Build their Beautiful Planned City State? Moreover, would they Spend all of their Money on Buying such a Mountain of Rocks, and not even have any Tools to Work with — not even a Train to Haul the Rocks to the Building Site?

09-06 [_] So, O Selected King, with Swangkeenomiks, the Mountains of Rocks would Belong to the New Righteous One-World GovernMint, along with all Sand, Gravel, Rivers of Water, Oil, Gas, Coal, and all other Natural Resources, including the Farm Lands and Ranches: beCause, **"The

New Righteous One-World Government" is the PEOPLES' Government, who will simply CLAIM ALL of their Natural Resources for the Benefit of EVERYONE; and therefore, no one will have to Buy any of those Things, including the TOOLS to Work with: beCause all of those Tools will also Belong to the New RIGHTEOUS One-World GovernMINT, which will have Plenty of Top-Quality Tools to Work with; but, it will not have a Billion Cars sitting in Parking Lots, waiting to be Sold to Ignorant Fools, who just Naturally Want to Pollute their Air, Water, and Land with STINK, Chemicals, and POISONS: beCause of not having any more Brains than a 6-year-old Child with Down's Syndrome! Indeed, if Bulldozers are Needed for Moving Dirt around, the New Righteous One-World Government will "Confiscate" as many Bulldozers as are Needed for Doing that Work, and even Produce many more Bulldozers for those **"Seven Great Armies of Working Soldiers!" (HOW to Provide a Way for Everyone to WORK: so as to Eliminate Poverty, Crimes, Drug Abuses, Prisons and Unnecessary Taxes!)**, Book 015, in Order to SPEED UP the Construction of those Beautiful Planned City States for EVERYONE in the World, who should have the Freedom to VOTE for The GOAT! {See www.Amazon.com for: **"Mark Twain Races for the PRESIDENCY!" (The 2020 Presidential Candidates Desperately Need Some STRONG Undefeatable COMPETITION!)**, Book 033.}

09-07 [_] Well, there will be a LOT of very Unhappy People with that Plan: beCause of Losing their Properties — that is, UNLESS we First Persuade them by Means of Reason and Logic that it is a Good Idea to make a Manmade Paradise for EVERYONE in the World, including their Poor Friends, Relatives, and Naaberz. Yes, even the "Enemies" also Need those Manmade Paradises, just to Change their Minds about the VALUE of Lives, including those of Wild Creatures, who also have a Right to LIVE, even as the American Bisons have a Right to Roam around on the Great Plains, once again, whereby they can Plant the Seeds of the Tall Grasses, which were up to 14 feet Tall during the 1800's, which have all but Vanished — Thanks to **"The Nature of CAPITALISM!" (A List of the EVILS of CAPITALISM!) By The Worldwide People's Revolution!®** Book 038. Indeed, it is much Better to Change their Minds by Reason and Logic, than by Bullets and Bombs. †‡

09-08 [_] O Selected King, just Exactly HOW could we Change the Minds of those Radical Muslims, who are Determined to Rule the World, and Force us to Bow Down to Mecca, 5 Times per Day?

09-09 [_] Well, we can Change their Minds toward us, just by letting them Rule the World! Yes, we can put the Responsibility on them to Govern their own little "Worlds" by Building their own Beautiful Planned City States, which they can Govern According to their own Elected Laws and Flexible Rules! Moreover, they will be Welcome to Elect a "High Priest" or Imam to Preach to them from **"The Great World TEMPLE of PEACE,"** in Jerusalem; and also Elect Kings to Govern each Islamic Nation, which Kings will Represent them in the New Righteous One-World Government. Therefore, they should be Happy with that Plan. After all, most Muslims are Presently EXTREMELY Poor, and do not even have Fresh Clean Air to Breathe, much less Pure Living Water to Drink, nor Wholesome Natural Foods to Eat, much less Secure Planned Cities to Live within, whereby they will not have to Worry about American Bombs falling on them, nor will Americans have to Worry about Russian Atomic and Hydrogen Bombs falling on them: because those Russians and Chinese will also Agree to Live in Manmade Paradises, and Live in PEACE, rather than Live in FEAR of American Hydrogen Bombs falling on them: beCause ALL such Aggressive Weapons will be done Away with, and Army Tanks will be Transformed into

(HOW all People can Prosper in a RIIT WAA, and Stop Polluting the Earth with Capitalist TRASH!)

Bulldozers, by Melting them Down, which will Require a LOT of Energy, which is now being Wasted by Cars and Trucks and ElecTRICK Power Plants. †‡ {See www.Amazon.com for: **"UNLIMITED ENERJEE 99 Percent Pollutions Free!" (HOW to Obtain FREE ElecTrickery, Worldwide!) By The Worldwide People's Revolution!®** Book 029.}

09-10 [_] O Elected King, just Exactly HOW will we go about Persuading those Chief Radical Muslims to come to **"The GREAT Worldwide TELEVISED Court HEARING,"** whereby they might Defend their Insane Beliefs? For Example, will the Leaders of ISIS (Israeli Secret Instigation Services) show their Faces at those Great Meetings of the Most Intelligent Minds? †§‡

09-11 [_] Well, they seem to know how to Communicate quite well with Modern Technology; and therefore, it should not be Difficult to Persuade them to come to the Meetings: beCause it will be in their Greatest Interest. After all, they have a "Just Cause" to Fight for, or else they would not be Fighting, right?

09-12 [_] Well, they might Imagine that they have a Just Cause, even as Adolf Hitler Imagined it; but, in Reality, they do not have a Just Cause. †§‡

09-13 [_] And, can you Prove that in a Courtroom? After all, there are Millions of People who say that Adolf Hitler did have a Just Cause for going to War, which can be Proven in a Courtroom. In Fact, I am one of those Millions of People, who will not Change my Mind, until it is Proven in a Courtroom with Law and Order, where ALL of the Evidence can be Presented on Worldwide Television, even to the Iranians, who also Sincerely Believe that Adolf Hitler had a Just Cause for going to War, and that Israelis STOLE the Land from the Palestinians, even as Europeans STOLE the Land from the American Indians, which can be Proven in a Courtroom! Therefore, if anyone is Seeking TRUE JUSTICE, it will have to Begin with the Whole Truth, and nothing but the Truth, including the Truth about Adolf Hitler, who has been Falsely Accused of Evil Things that he was not Responsible for. Indeed, it was Zionist Jews who were in Charge of the Concentration Camps during World War 2 — NOT Adolf Hitler! Yes, that can be Proven in a Courtroom, and will be Proven, if I am in Charge of it. {See www.Amazon.com for: **"LIGHTNING STRIKES Versus Lightning Bugs!" (HOW you can Become Moderately RICH, without Telling any Lies nor Selling any Trash!)**, Book 074, which tells all about that Great Meeting of the Most Intelligent Minds, which will Naturally Include those Honest Iranians, who have Collected a Mountain of Evidence to Justify the Actions of Adolf Hitler, who was NOT the Cigar-chomping Whiskey-drinking Gluttonous DRUNKARD across the English Channel, who was a Good Blabbermouth; but, he was NOT an Honest Person by any Means, let alone a RIGHTEOUS Man, even as Saint Joseph Stalin was not a Righteous Man, and yet **"The Divided States of United Lies"** took his Side during the War, after Knowing for a Fact that he had already Murdered MILLIONS of his own Fellow Russians, who were known as White CHRISTIANS. In Fact, the History Channel Reported that he had some 40 to 50 Million White Russian Christians put to Death during his Reign of Terror, and that it was Covered Up by the United States Federal Government for more than 40 Years! So, you might Wonder WHY? Well, that is beCause Saint Joseph Stalin had RED JEW Connections: beCause Russian Communism was Founded by Lying Red Jews, even as American Capitalism was Founded by Lying Red Jews: beCause they Work on both Sides, and they even Supported Adolf Hitler during the War: beCause it was PROFITABLE for them, even as they still Support both Sides and all Sides of the Present Wars: beCause they are in the Banking

Business, which Collects TRILLIONS of Dollars from Ignorant FOOLS, and for doing almost nothing! Yes, and YOU Love it, huh? †§‡

09-14 [_] O Selected King, I have Heard that Americans were in a Great Bankers Depression during the 1930's, whereby there was no Money for Buying nor Investing in anything, in spite of the Fact that much Work Needed Doing — such as Constructing the Interstate Highway System — beCause those Rich Edomite Bankers were HORDING their Billions of Dollars in their Banks, while a hundred-million Americans were Unemployed, and Hungry People were standing in Long Soup Lines, by the thousands, all Day long, waiting to get a Bowl of Soup with a Bean or 2 in it: beCause of being Jobless Graduates of the Public School of Ignorant FOOLS, which did not Teach to them anything about a New RIGHTEOUS One-World Government. (See Verse 01-01.) Indeed, those Bankers Horded their Countless Billions of Dollars, while Americans Suffered without Jobs — that is, until World War 2 broke out, when Japan Attacked Pearl Harbor, in Hawaii; and then, behold, within a Week or less, those same Greedy Selfish Bankers Suddenly came up with BILLIONS of Dollars for Building Millions of Airplanes, Army Tanks, Army Trucks, Army Jeeps, Boats, Submarines, Aircraft Carriers, Big Guns, Rifles, Ammunitions, Grenades, Mines, Bombs, Uniforms, Helmets, Gas Masks, Mess Kits, K-rations, Trainloads of Cigarettes, Candies, Cokes, and whatever was Necessary for going to WAR: beCause it was PROFITABLE for them, who Collected Billions of Dollars in USURY Payments, which they called INTEREST on the Loans, which most Americans have never Objected to Paying: beCause they are in LOVE with those Holy Edomite Bankers, who are the GOOD Guys! Yes, they are the People with MONEY! Indeed, what in this World could anyone Do without LOTS and LOTS of MONEY? Therefore, the Borrower is Happy to get some Money from those Friendly Bankers; and then the Borrower is DEPRESSED by having to Repay his Loan with Interest, whereby he Turns to Drinking Alcoholic Beverages, just to Sooth his Nerves and Appease his ANGER: beCause, if he Manages to Earn some Money by Hook or Crook, the Government will be Riding on his Back to Collect some TAXES. Therefore, all such Tax Slaves and Usury Slaves are just Naturally DRIVEN to Drinking, Using Drugs, or doing something to Try to ESCAPE from the PRESSURES of Living in a Capitalist Dog-Eat-Dog World, which Drives many of them Completely INSANE, whereby they begin to Imagine that EVIL Things are GOOD Things, including those Hateful WARS! Yes, they even Seek to Justify those Stinking Noisy Polluting Cars, Vans, Pickups, Buses, Trucks, Tractors, Airplanes, Lawnmowers, Chainsaws, and all such DANGEROUS EVIL Things, which KILL more than 20,000,000 People per Year, Worldwide, even with Lung Diseases, which is more People than were Killed on Average per Year during World War 2, while tens of Millions of People are Wounded by those Cars, Vans, Pickups, Buses, Trucks, Tractors, Lawnmowers, Chainsaws, Motorboats, and so on: beCause they are Inventions of the Synagogue of SATAN! Indeed, those Evil Things were not Needed for True Prosperity, even as you have Proven in: **"The Nature of CAPITALISM!" (A List of the EVILS of CAPITALISM!)**, Book 038. Yes, those Poor Wretched Deceived Ignorant FOOLS Seek to Justify those Lying Red Jews, who are the Inventors of all such Abominations, which God HATES: beCause, they not only Wound and Kill Millions of People; but, they Cause Various Kinds of Sicknesses and Diseases: beCause they are Unnatural, while the Farts of a Horse never Killed anyone, even though a few People have been Killed by Horses; but, only if they were Mean to them, or did not know how to Manage them Properly. Nevertheless, my Point is Clear — the Interest Slaves are at the Mercies of Edomite Bankers, who are the Chief Bank Robbers and Slave Masters, and "Nigger Jim and Huck Finn" Know for a Fact that that is the Truth, which can be Proven in a Courtroom! †§‡

(HOW all People can Prosper in a RIIT WAA, and Stop Polluting the Earth with Capitalist TRASH!)

09-15 [_] Well, my Friend, no matter how many Times that you might Tell those Tax Slaves, Interest Slaves, Insurance Slaves, Drug Slaves, Sex Slaves, and Work Slaves all such Truths, they will just Naturally Refuse to Agree with you: beCause they have their Heads STUCK in one or the other of those 2 Stinking Holes in **"The BIG White OUTHOUSE on the Not-so-Biblical Capitol DUNGHILL!" (The Chief Sins of the Divided States of United Lies!)**, Book 023, which they Refuse to Study: beCause they Know for a Fact that they do not have a Leg to Stand on in a Courtroom with Law and Order, whereby True Justice might be Served to ALL of the People, Worldwide, including those Bombed Out People in Laos, Cambodia, Vietnam, Korea, Japan, Germany, Iraq, Afghanistan, Syria, and wherever the Long Arms of Capitalist Tyrants have Reached, even to the Jungles of Ecuador and Brazil, where the Capitalist "Niggers" Ruined the Land and Rivers for the Natives: beCause of their GREED! †§‡

09-16 [_] So, O Selected King, will Swangkeenomiks not also Produce GREEDY Selfish People? Will we not be Reading about them on the Internet, and Watching Evil Reports about them on YouTube Videos?

— Chapter 10 —

Will Swangkeenomiks Produce Greedy Selfish People?

10-01 [_] The Answer is: Of course NOT! How can Swangkeenomiks Produce any Evils? ‡

10-02 [_] O Selected King, are you Sure that certain Cunning Edomites will not figure out HOW to take Advantage of the Masses of People, since they still Control the News Media? After all, he who Controls the Messages, Controls the Masses: beCause of Controlling their Thinking. ‡

10-03 [_] Well, they do not Control how many Copies of my Inspired Books that you can Reproduce and Sell for a Reasonable Profit, and Keep 90% of the Net Profits for your own Prosperity. Therefore, even if they Manage to Cut Off my Good Books from all Normal Book Stores, you can be Wise, and Spread the Good News that I Teach, whereby we, the People, can get into Control of the News Media, which will be mostly by Means of Telephones, whereby Good News can Spread just as Fast as Evil News; and thus, at Last, the Good News will WIN: beCause it is Supported by Provable Truths, while the Evil News has nothing to Support it.

10-04 [_] O Selected King, I say that you are just another Communist in a Different Snake's Skin, whereby you have Deceived Millions of Ignorant People, who are not Aware of the Facts. (Please Check the following Boxes with Statements that you Agree with.)

    A-[_] There are not Enough Mountains of Rocks in this World of Wonders, whereby everyone in the World could Obtain a Beautiful Stone Dome Home Complex with a one-acre Organic Garden. §

    B-[_] There is not Enough Water in the whole World for Watering all such Gardens. §

SWANGKEENOMIKS Rules the Roost!

C-[_] There is not Enough Gasoline to Power the Necessary Tools for Building Millions of **"GLORIOUS Swanky Hotels Castles and Fortresses!" (Beautiful Planned City States for WISE Intelligent Well-Educated People with Common Sense and Good Understanding!)**, Book 019: because we have to use that gas in our Cars, until it is all Wasted; and then there will be Zero Gas for Building anything but Mud Huts in Africa, and Bamboo Huts in Brazil. Indeed, there will not even be Diesel for Tractors for Farming the Fields. Even now it Requires 1,000 Calories of Energy to Produce 1 Calorie of Food. †§‡§§

D-[_] There is not Enough Money for Building all such Fortresses. §

E-[_] There are not Enough Working Soldiers to do that much Work. §

F-[_] There are not Enough Machines for Cutting and Polishing so many Rocks for so many Beautiful Stone Dome Homes, Workshops, nor Sales Shops. §

G-[_] Robots cannot Lay Heavy Stones Properly. †§‡

H-[_] Men do not like to Work with their Hands and Backs. Indeed, they might get Tired, and not be Able to Figure Out HOW to Rest. §§

I-[_] The Indians would rather Live in Teepees and Wigwams. §

J-[_] There is not Enough Space in Deserts for Building those Swanky Fortresses. §

K-[_] We would be Defenseless without Atomic and Hydrogen Bombs, even if we Built Millions of Swanky Fortresses, Worldwide. §

L-[_] Lots of Laughs! You need to Study: **"The Right Design for Living!" (A List of Great Advantages for Building Beautiful Planned City States!)**, Book 012.

M-[_] All of the Money will end up in the Hands of Greedy Selfish Red Jew Bankers. §

N-[_] Not even Jesus Christ would Approve of Building Swanky Fortresses: because they would Solve too many Problems, whereby People would never get Sick, Diseased, Killed in Car Accidents, Tornadoes, Floods, Fires, Hurricanes, Earthquakes, Tsunamis, nor other Natural Disasters, which might Cause them to REPENT. §

O-[_] There are not Enough OPTIONS to Choose from, if there are only 7 Basic Kinds of Swanky Fortresses with thousands of Varieties among them, according to their Religious and Political Beliefs. §

P-[_] There is not Enough Technology to Accomplish such a Massive Project. §

Q-[_] The Queens in Swanky Palaces will not Like them: beCause they will Prefer to Live in Used Vans down by the River of Filthiness with Fat Chris Farley, who has nothing but Macaroni and Imitation Cheese to Eat with Mercury-laden Fishes. §

R-[_] The Resurrection will not be Necessary: because everyone will be Reincarnated into Families who Live in Swanky Fortresses, which will make the Unholy Bible Obsolete. §

(HOW all People can Prosper in a RIIT WAA, and Stop Polluting the Earth with Capitalist TRASH!)

S-[_] The World Bank, the International Monetary Fund, and SINator Warmonger will be made Unhappy by Swanky Fortresses: because there will be no one to Loan Money to. §

T-[_] Temptations will become Impossible, whereby People will not be Tested for their Faith in some Imaginary God. §

U-[_] Swangkeenomiks is Utter MADNESS: beCause Poverty will be done Away with, whereby it will become Impossible for Rich People to be Glorified by Assisting Poor People, who are known as PhilanthroPISTS. §

V-[_] Queen Victoria will Envy us, which will be Bad: because Envy is Bad. Therefore, it will be Wise of us to Live in Used Vans down by the River of Filthiness with Fat Farley.§

W-[_] No one will be Able to Envy anyone, if we Build Swanky PALACES for everyone, whereby that Deadly Sin will have to be Crossed Off of the List of 7 Deadliest Sins, which List begins with Pride, and ends with Gluttony and Slothfulness. §

X-[_] X-amount of People are Insane, and will likely Die for it: because no one will Care for them. §

Y-[_] Janet Yellen and Ben Bernanke will not be able to Repeat Allan Greenspan's Speeches, slightly modified, which will Prove to be too Em-bare-assing for them. §§

Z-[_] Zebras will not be Able to Understand Swangkeenomiks: beCause of being Double-minded, which will make Swangkeenomiks BAD, even as the *Bible* is Bad, if you only Study it for Learning HOW to Murder Innocent People like Abel and Jesus. §

10-05 [_] O Selected King, I only found one Box to Check with an X.

10-06 [_] O Selected King, if you are a Communist, so were the Disciples of Jesus Christ, according to *the Book of Acts*. Therefore, I Suggest that whomever Falsely Accuses you of being a Communist — after Plainly Teaching that Free Enterprise is GOOD, and that any Person or Family may have his or her or their own Home-craft Workshop and Sales Shop — should be brought to Court in Shackles and Chains, and made to Prove that you are a Communist, or else be Whipped with 40 Lashes of a Bull Whip. †‡

10-07 [_] O Selected King, will your New "RIGHTEOUS" One-World GovernMint not "Confiscate," or STEAL the Patents of Rich People — such as Apple Computers, which you will Reproduce by the Billions: so that everyone in the World can have a Good Computer for FREE? Is that not WORSE than Communism?

10-08 [_] Well, I have already said, somewhere, that anyone may Sell my Inspired Books, and use 90% of the Net Profits for BUYING all such Computers and Wide Flat-screen TV's, whereby I can use my 10% of the Net Profits for Buying all such Computers for Poor People who are Deprived of them. So, does that Sound so BAD to you? Did the Communists do anything like that? Did the Communists ever Propose any of the Good Things that I have Proposed? Did the Capitalists ever Propose such Good Things? NO, Absolutely NOT: beCause they are Possessed by the EVIL Spirits of GREED, LUST, SELFISHNESS, PRIDE, GLUTTONY, DRUNKENNESS, ENVY, HATE, STRIFE, MALICE, MURDER, and WAR: beCause they are of the Synagogue of Satan! Yes, it can be Proven in a Courtroom! †‡

10-09 [_] O Selected King, it does Appear to me that **"SWANGKEENOMIKS Rules the Roost!" (HOW all People can Prosper in a RIIT WAA, and Stop Polluting the Earth with Capitalist TRASH!) By The Worldwide People's Revolution!® Book 039.**

10-10 [_] Well, I have been Trying to tell you that my Master Plan is a Revelation from the Master Farmer, himself, and that no one can Improve on it: beCause it is a RIGHTEOUS Plan, which Provides True Justice for ALL Peoples, Worldwide. {See www.Amazon.com for: **"The CONSTITUTION for the New RIGHTEOUS One-World GovernMINT!" (HOW all Peoples can get True Justice, and Celebrate the Great Year of JUBILEE!), Book 016, plus: "The Great World TEMPLE of PEACE!" (The Glory of Jerusalem Arise Again!) By The Worldwide People's Revolution!® Book 017.**

— Chapter 11 —

Will Swangkeenomiks CRASH the Great False Economy?

11-01 [_] A Few People in the World will Naturally See the Crash of the Great False Economy as a BAD Thing, while the Masses of People will See it as a GOOD Thing; but, only IF Swangkeenomiks Rules the Roost, whereby they can all become Moderately RICH, and in all Ways. Most of all, they will Greatly Appreciate the Fresh Clean Air, the Pure Living Water, the Wholesome Natural Foods, the Natural Clothing — such as Silk, Linen, Hemp, and Cotton — and the Secure Fireproof, Mouse-proof, Termite-proof, Rot-proof, Paint-proof, Hail-proof, Tornado-proof, Insurance-proof, Tax-proof Houses within Extremely Secure Swanky Fortresses. {See www.Amazon.com for: **"Terrorists Beware that your Days are Numbered!" (HOW to Bring those Terrorist Attacks to a Screeching HALT!), Book 043, plus: "The LUSCIOUS All-Mineral Organic Method of Gardening!" (HOW to Grow DELICIOUS Satisfying Foods for Potential Kingz and Kweenz in Swanky PALACES!), Book 021, plus: "Poverty Hunger Riots Strikes Brutalities Election Deceptions and Civil Wars!" (The High Price that we Earthlings have Paid for Leaving the Good Land!) By The Worldwide People's Revolution!® B-014.**}

11-02 [_] So, O Selected King, just Exactly HOW will we go about making "Pure Living Water" to Drink?

11-03 [_] Well, that is Explained in one of the above Books that I Referred you to, which is Worthy to be Repeated again. However, if I do Repeat it, someone will be Complaining about my "Redundant Literature," which seems to be Boring to them. After all, X-amount of People say, "I have Heard that same Song before," and then, under their Breaths, they say: "... and I do not Want

(HOW all People can Prosper in a RIIT WAA, and Stop Polluting the Earth with Capitalist TRASH!)

to Hear it again," even though they will do Well to Remind themselves of just HOW such Things as Pure Living Water is Obtained, and ONLY at: **"GLORIOUS Swanky Hotels Castles and Fortresses!" (Beautiful Planned City States for WISE Intelligent Well-Educated People with Common Sense and Good Understanding!) By The Worldwide People's Revolution!®**, Book 019, which has the Best Plan for Providing Pure Living Water for People, Animals, Fruit Trees, and Luscious All-Mineral Organic Gardens: beCause every Living Thing NEEDS Pure Living Water, except for maybe Algeegaaterz, Slugz, Snakes, Lizards, Rats and Lying Politicians. †§‡

11-04 [_] So, O Selected King, how Long will it be before you Obtain a Master Index to all of your Inspired Books: so that we do not Waste too much Time Searching for Key Verses of Important Information?

11-05 [_] Well, when the Great False Economy CRASHES, I will not have much else to Do, except to make that Master Index. After all, my Inspired Books will, without any Doubt, CRASH that Great False Economy, which is otherwise known as *the Fall of Babylon,* which you can read about in *the Book of Revelation.* Indeed, I have written the New MAGNIFIED Version of it, somewhere; but, right now, I cannot Remember just WHERE it is Found: beCause of not having that Master Index. Therefore, I am now Tempted to make up a NEW Version of it, just in Case that it might be more Enlightening in the Light of the Truths that are Found within this Inspired Book, which might Change it a bit from the other Version.

11-06 [_] O Selected King, if your New MAGNIFIED Version (NMV) were Inspired by GOD, it would be Perfect just as it is: beCause it is Impossible to Improve on a Perfectly Cut and Polished Gemstone. †§‡

11-07 [_] And would that be WHY the Hope Diamond was Recut and slightly Reshaped by Harry Winston between 1949 and 1958? (See *Wikipedia* for the Details for the *Hope Diamond*.)

11-08 [_] O Elected King, you certainly do not Object to Flattering yourself about your Beautiful Gems of Provable Truths, do you?

11-09 [_] Well, if no one else can Recognize the Beauty of those Gems of Truths, then I must Glorify them with my "Flatteries": beCause no one else seems to be Able to, or at least not Willing to, which seems to be very Strange to me: beCause I can Recognize those Gems of Truths, even before they are Cut and Polished, which is WHY that I have "red" the *Bible* no less than 20 Times from Cover to Cover: beCause it Contains a LOT of Unpolished "Gemstones" from Cover to Cover. Yes, I could write a thousand or more Books from single Verses, which only Need to be MAGNIFIED! †

11-10 [_] O Selected King, I just LOVE your New Magnified Versions of the *Scriptures,* which are very Rich with Metaphors and Similes. In Fact, I can hardly wait to read **"The New MAGNIFIED Version of the Book of MORMON!" (The Story of the White and Dark Indians in the Americas!)**, Book 040, which is likely going to Sell a hundred Times more Copies than the Original Book of Mormon! Moreover, I do Hope to God that you Write another *New Magnified Version of Revelation 16—21,* just for our Enlightenment: beCause I Know that you will Greatly Improve on it, even as you always do with New Magnified Versions, which you seem to be Able to Rearrange in such a Way as to make those Versions Fit into whatever your Beliefs are, even if your Beliefs Change ever so Slightly, even as they have done over the past 40 Years, whereby you are Growing in Grace and in True Nolij, which is Far Superior to any knowledge that we might Learn in the Public School of Ignorant Fools. (See Verse 01-01.)

A-[_] Then I Heard an Awesome Voice from the Temple in the Sky, which said to the Seven Angels who have Power Over the Whole Earth: "Go your Ways, and Pour Out on the Earth the Seven Symbolical Bowls that Contain the Wrath of God," who should really not be very Angry with People: beCause he could Appear to them in the Sky, and thus Change their Minds about his Laws of Life, even as he Appeared to the Ancient Israelites on Mount Sinai, according to the Jewish Myth, which Changed their Minds for 2 or 3 Days. ‡

B-[_] And thus the First Angel left the Temple in the Sky, and Poured Out his Bowl on the Earth; and thus Horrible, Malignant Sores broke out on everyone who had the Identifying Mark of the Beastly Government that Ruled the World by Controlling the Money Supply, and on whomever Worshiped his Image that Speaks, which is otherwise known as the Television, which Advertises all Kinds of Vain Things, whereby Trillions of Dollars-worth of Drugs and Stinking Noisy Vehicles are Sold.

C-[_] Then the Second Angel Poured Out his Bowl on the Seas, and thus the Oceans became Poisoned, even as the Morticians will Embalm Dead Bodies with Extremely Toxic Poisons, which will Replace the Blood in Corpses; and thus, every Kind of Creature in the Seas Died from the Poisons and Pollutions, whereby even many Great Whales Beached themselves, and Died, while many Creatures Died from the Acid Rains, which Weakened the Shells on Shell Fishes, which are made of Calcium and other Minerals. ‡

D-[_] Then the Third Angel Poured Out his Bowl on the Rivers and Springs of Waters, and they also became like Blood, which no one Wanted to Drink: beCause of the Poisons, which also Killed a third of the Life in the Rivers, Worldwide. And I Heard the Angel, who had Authority Over all Waters, saying: "You are Justified to Govern the Whole Earth, O Holy One, who was from the Beginning, who still Lives, and who is yet to Come on the Earth: because you have Sent these Judgments on the Disobedient Selfish Sinners: because they Shed the Blood of your Holy People, and even your Prophets; and therefore, you have Given to them Blood to Drink: because it is their Just Reward." However, the Problem with that Kind of "Justice" is the Fact that Innocent Little Children often have to Drink the Water from the Lead-filled Water Pipes: beCause their Poor Parents cannot Afford to Import Pure Water from Antarctica. ‡

E-[_] And I Heard a Voice from the Altar, saying: "Yes, O Ruling God — the Almighty One, who Believes in Liberty and Justice for all Creatures — your Judgments are True and Just, which no Honest Person can Rightly Deny." And he was being very Sarcastic. †§‡§§

F-[_] Then the Fourth Angel Poured Out his Bowl on the Sunstar, causing it to Scorch everyone with Great Heat, as with Burning Fire in a Forest, whereby only those Wise People and their Animals, who kept themselves in Caves and in Stone Dome Homes with very Thick Stone Walls could Survive it. Indeed, everyone who was not Living Securely was Burned by that Blast of Heat, and thus they Cursed the Name of God, who had Control Over all of these Plagues, which are Punishments upon the Wicked People for their Evil

Deeds: because they Refused to Repent of all such Evil Deeds, whereby they might have Turned Back to God, and even Praised him for having Mercy on them by Sending to them the Man with the Spirit of Elijah, who Warned them to Build Proper Planned City States. However, most of them had Developed a Doomsday Attitude, whereby they Preferred to Die, than to get their Lazy Asses to WORK, and do Constructive and Useful Things with their Time, Money, Materials, and Energy, rather than Waste it all on their Foolishness. ‡

G-[_] Then the Fifth Angel Poured Out his Bowl on the Government of the Beast, which was Plunged into Great Darkness, whereby none of the Leaders could Present any Reasonable Solutions for Solving their Perplexing Problems, even though his Subjects Ground their Teeth with Anguish, and Gnawed their Tongues for their Great Pains, while they Cursed the God of Heaven for their Pains, Itches and Sores: because they Refused to Blame themselves for their Curses, and would not Repent of their Evil Deeds, and thus Turn Back to God, their Savior and Best Friend. Indeed, they Insisted that their Abominations were Good, in spite of being the Causes for many Deaths among them, and much Suffering. Yes, it was as if they were made Spiritually Blind, so that they could not See the Truth of it: beCause of the Darkness of Ignorance. Moreover, they Refused to Study the Inspired Words of Provable Truths, which were Delivered to them by the Man with the Spirit of Elijah.

H-[_] Then the Sixth Angel Poured Out his Bowl on the Great Euphrates River, so that it Dried Up, whereby the Kings from the East might March their Great Armies to the West, whereby they might Conquer the Land of Israel, which was the Cause for all of those Plagues and Curses: beCause they were the Chiefs among Men, who Controlled the Money Supply, the News Reporters, the Drug Industries, the Book Publishing Companies, the Weapons Manufacturers, the Chemical Corporations, and all Kinds of Abominations. ‡

I-[_] Then I saw three Evil Spirits, which Looked like Frogs, Leaping from the Mouths of the Dragon, the Beast, and the False Prophet. Yes, they are Demoniac Spirits, who Work Marvelous Things, and go out to all of the Rulers of the World, in Order to Gather them Together for a Great Battle against the Supreme Ruler, himself, who will Consume them with Devouring Fire: because he is the Almighty God, even the Creator of this Heaven and Earth, who says: "Behold, I will Come as Unexpectedly as a Thief during the Darkness of your Ignorance! Therefore, Blest are all People who are Watching for me, who Keep their Robes White, and their Consciences Clean: so that they will not have to Walk around Naked and Ashamed of themselves for their Sins." But, the Preachers and Teachers Failed to Explain to them what all of their Sins are, whereby they did not know what to Repent of. Indeed, they did not even Realize that SIN is the Transgression of God's Laws! ‡

J-[_] And the Demonic Spirits Gathered all of the Rulers of the Perverse Nations and their Armies to a Place with the Hebrew Name of Armageddon, for a Great Battle: because they Love those Gory Bloody Wars, rather than Settle their Differences in a Courtroom with Law and Order, even as all Righteous People would: beCause the Sword of Truths cannot be Defeated by any Means. Therefore, whomever has the Whole Truth on his Side is the Victor, and all other Wise People will Humbly Submit to that Divine Sword of Provable Truths, whereby everyone gets True Justice. {See: **"The Swanky Sword of Divine Truths!" (The Most Powerful Weapon in the Whole Universe!)** Book 067.

K-[_] Then the Seventh Angel Poured Out his Bowl into the Air, and a Mighty Shout came from the Throne within the Great World Temple of Peace, in Jerusalem, saying: "It is Finished! The End of Confusion has Come!" {See: **"The END of CONFUSION!" (The Great CELEBRATION of the Magnificent Wedding of the Most Humble Honest Nations, and the Grand Year of JUBILEE!) By The Worldwide People's Revolution!®**, Book 050, which is an Amazing Book!}

L-[_] Then the Lightning Struck, and the Thunder Clapped, and Great Thick Clouds of Darkness Rolled across the Sky; and a Great Earthquake Struck the Whole Earth, and Shook the Mountains unto the Foundations thereof — even the Worst Earthquake since People were Placed on the Earth by the Gods from other Worlds, whereby all Tall Towers and High Walls Fell to the Ground, unless they were of the same Angles as the Great Pyramids in the World, which is the same Angle that all Tall Stone Walls should be within Beautiful Planned City States, which can be used Wisely for Building Arcades of Stone Wind Generators for Free Electricity for everyone. ‡ (See page 5 for the Rough Drawings.)

M-[_] Moreover, the Great City of Confusion was Divided into three Sections, and the Cities of many Nations Fell into Heaps of Rubble, whereby many People were Crushed to Death. Yes, God Remembered all of the Sins of Babylon, which is Confusion; and thus he made her to Drink from the Cup that was Filled with the Bitter Wine of his Fierce Wrath; and thus every Island of the Seas Disappeared under the Tidal Waves, and all of the Mountains were Leveled Out, and the Continents were Joined back Together again, even as they were in the Beginning, whereby their was only one Great Ocean.

N-[_] Then there was a Terrible Hailstorm, with Stones weighing as much as 70 to 100 Pounds, which Fell from the Dark and Awesome Sky onto everything below them: so that whomever was not Living in a Cave, or in a Properly-built Stone Dome Home, was Killed by the Hail, which Leveled many Houses, and Killed many Animals. Therefore, the People who Remained, Cursed God: because of the Terrible Plague of the Hailstorm, which Stripped every Tree of its Branches, and left nothing but Stumps, even in the Great Forests.

O-[_] Then one of the Seven Angels, who had Poured Out his Bowl, came over and Spoke with me, saying: "Come with me, and I will Show to you the Judgment that is going to Come on the Mother of Prostitutes and the Producer of Abominations, who Rules Over many Nations and Great Waters by Reason of the Fact that she Controls the Money Supply, whereby she can Oppress whomever does not Play with her in the Bed of Lusts, and become Addicted to her Drugs. Yes, she Produces many Criminals, and is Identified by her many Hateful Weapons. Yes, the Kings of the World have Committed Spiritual Adultery with her, and have Worshiped their Possessions; and the People who belong to this World, who have been made Drunk by her Deceptive Wine, Vainly Imagine that she will Endure Forever; but, behold, she will Fall, and Great shall be the Fall thereof."

P-[_] So, the Angel took me in the Spirit, into the Future, into the Wilderness; and there I saw a Woman sitting on a Scarlet Beast, which had Seven Heads and Ten Horns, and Blasphemies against God were written all over it. Moreover, the Woman Wore Purple and Scarlet Clothing, and Beautiful Jewelry made of Gold and Precious Gemstones and Pearls, even while Multitudes of Poor People Suffered in their States of Extreme Poverty. Indeed, in her Hand she held a Golden Goblet full of Obscenities and Blasphemies and the Impurities of her Vile Ways, even though she Imagined that she would Live Forever! Furthermore, a Mysterious Name was written on her Forehead: "Babylon, the Great Mother and Producer of Prostitutes and Abominations throughout the World." {FOOTNOTE: If you Doubt that **"The Divided States of United Lies!" (The so-called "United States of North America" in Disguise!)**, Book 058, is not a Producer of Abominations, you should Study such Enlightening Books as: *Silent Spring,* by Rachel Carson, and Related Books. In Fact, the Edomites come up with some 3,000+ New Chemical Abominations on Average, each Year: beCause it is very Profitable for the Rich Hogs, who could care less about the Environment, our Good Health, and the Future Children with all Kinds of Unnecessary Diseases — except that some of them might be the very Inventors of such Abominations, who are getting Recycled for Learning their Lessons. ‡}

Q-[_] Yes, I could See that she was Drunk with Pride, and also Drunk with the Blood of God's Holy People, who were Witnesses for Jesus. Therefore, I stared at her in Complete Amazement, Wondering what she Symbolized. Indeed, I could See that she was Drunk with Pride — and also Drunk with the Blood of God's Holy People, who were Witnesses for Jesus, who Taught the same Great Truths that he Taught, and were Persecuted for it.

R-[_] And the Angel said, "Why are you so Amazed by her? Do you not See her Nakedness under her Robe of Deceptions and Lies? Well, I will tell you the Truth about her, and Reveal the Mysteries of this Hateful Woman and the Beast with Seven Heads and Ten Horns, on which she Rides with Great Pride. Indeed, the Beast that you saw was once Alive; but, now it is Dead and Gone Away; and yet he will soon come up again from the Bottomless Pit, and go into Eternal Punishment and Damnation for his Evil Deeds and Deceptive Words, which Punishment is called Perdition. And the People, who belong to Satan, who presently Governs this World of Woes and all Evil Nations, whose Names were not Written in the Book of Life from before the Foundation of this World was made, will be Amazed at the Reappearance of this Beast, who was and is not, and yet he still Lives, who had Died, but is still Alive. Yes, this calls for the Mind of Good Understanding, and the Wisdom of King Solomon.

S-[_] "The Seven Heads of the Beast Represent the Seven Hills from which the Woman Rules the Ungodly Nations, which also Represent Seven Kingdoms. Yes, Five of those Kingdoms have already Fallen, and the Sixth one now Reigns, and the Seventh one is yet to Come; but, his Reign will be much more Brief, being the Last Great Kingdom with Demonic Powers. The Scarlet Beast that was, but is no longer, is the Eighth Kingdom. He is like the other Seven in some Ways; but, he too is Headed for Perdition: because the Masses of People within that Unholy Kingdom will not Agree to Establish a New Righteous One-World Government: because of Fearing it, being very Superstitious and Vain People, who are Unwilling to Prove anything, much less Hold Tightly to All that is GOOD. †‡

T-[_] The Ten Horns of the Beast are Ten Kings of European Nations, who have not as yet Risen to Power, who will Agree to Establish a New Righteous One-World Government; and they will be Appointed to their Kingdoms for one Brief Moment of Time to Reign with the Man who will Falsely be called the Beast: because of using the Names of Beasts to tell his Stories, and to Teach his Provable Truths. Yes, they will all Agree to give to him their Power and Authority: because he will Promise to make all of them Moderately Rich with Beautiful Palaces. Therefore, they will Band Together, in Order to go to War against the Beast that shall Arise from the Midst of the Great Seas; but, the Lamb of God will Defeat them with his Sword of Truths: because he is the Supreme Ruler, even the KING of Kings and the RULER of Rulers. Moreover, his Called and Faithful Servants will be with him when he Returns with Power and Great Glory as the Lion of the Tribe of Judah."

U-[_] Then I Looked at that Beast, who Arose from the Midst of the Seas, and behold, he was the Worst of all of the Beasts: because he Looked like an Innocent Lamb, and Spoke like a Deceptive Snake with a Split Tongue, and Acted like a Fiery Dragon, which Produced many Abominations by his Arts and Crafts, whereby he Destroyed much Life on the Earth. Then the Angel said to me, "The Waters where the Mother of Prostitutes is Ruling from Represent the Masses of People from every Nation and Language, while the Scarlet Beast and his Ten Horns shall all Hate the Old Whore, whereby they will Strip her Naked, Eat her Flesh, and Burn her Remains with Fire: because God has put a Plan into their Minds, even a Plan that will Carry Out his Purposes, one of which is to Teach all of the People that they must Learn, Believe, Love, and Obey all of God's Commandments, which are not Grievous. Therefore, those Wise Kings and their People will Agree to Give their Authority to the Scarlet Beast, and thus the Words of God will be Fulfilled. And this Woman whom you saw in your Vision Represents the Great City of New York, which Rules Over the Kingdoms of the World by Controlling the Money Supply." ‡

V-[_] And after all of that, I saw another Angel coming down from Heaven with Great Authority, and the Earth grew Bright with his Splendor: because he was the Angel of Light and Enlightenment; and he gave a Mighty Shout, saying: "Babylon has Fallen, Confusion has Fallen — even that Great City has Fallen, and her Financial Kingdom has Collapsed. Indeed, she has become a Home for Demon Spirits of Lusts and Greed. Yes, she is a Hideout for every Foul and Mean Spirit, and a Place of Refuge for every Stinking Vulture and Filthy Buzzard, who Lives on the Rotting Flesh of Honest Hardworking People; and every Loathsome and Dreadful Animal Lives in her: because she is a City of Criminals, and the Producer of Abominations, whereby all of the Deceived Nations have Fallen with her: because of the Poisonous Wine of her Evil Concoctions. Indeed, the Kings of the World have Committed Spiritual Adultery with her: because of their Desires for her Extravagant Luxuries, whereby certain Merchants of the World have Grown Rich with the False Riches."

W-[_] Then I Heard another Voice calling from the Sky, saying: "Come Away from her, O my People, Come Out from the Midst of her, and do not Touch any of her Abominations, lest you should be Partakers of her Sins, whereby you will be Punished with her: because her Sins are Piled Up into the Sky, you might say; but, God will Remember her Evil Deeds, and will Reward her Justly. Yes, he will say to those Ten Great Kings: 'Do to her as she has Done to others. Double her Penalties for all of her Evil Deeds, and Burn her with Fire. Indeed, she Brewed a Cup of Terror during September 11, so Brew twice as much for her. She Glorified herself with Abominations, and Lived in Luxury. Therefore, Match it now with Torments and Sorrows. She Boasted in her Heart, saying: "I am a Queen among the Nation, who have Nursed on my Breasts; and therefore, I Sit as a Queen on my Royal

Throne, and shall not be Removed from it. Indeed, I am no Helpless Old Lady, and I have no Reason to Mourn for my Wickedness: because I have Covered myself with Good Deeds." Therefore, all of these Plagues will Overtake her during a single Day of Woes — even Death and Mourning and Famine! Yes, she will be Completely Consumed by Devouring Fire: because the Supreme Ruling God who Judges her is Mightier than she.' And thus the Kings of the World, who Committed Adultery with her and Enjoyed her Great Luxuries, will Mourn and Lament for her as they see the Smoke of her Torment Arising from her Charred Remains. Yes, they will Stand at a Safe Distance, being Terrified by her Great Torment. And thus they will Cry Out: 'How Terrible, how Awful it has been for you, O Babylon, you Great City of Confusion! In a single Moment of Time, God's Judgment has come on you, and you could not Escape.'

X-[_] "Indeed, the Merchants of the World will Weep and Mourn for her: because there will be no one left Alive in that Great City of Confusion to Buy their Merchandise anymore. Yes, she Bought Great Quantities of Gold, Silver, Jewels, and Pearls; fine Linen, Purple Cloth, Silk, and Scarlet Cloth — even Things made of Fragrant Thyine Wood, Ivory Goods, and Objects made of Expensive Woods; as well as Bronze, Iron, Marbles, Granites, and Onyxes. She also Bought much Cinnamon, Spices, Incense, Myrrh, Aloes, Frankincense, Nutmeg, Pepper Corns, Wines, Olive Oil, Fine Flour, Wheat, Cattle, Sheeps, Goats, Horses, Wagons, and Human Slaves, whereby she Grew Rich with the False Riches. Therefore, the Luxurious Things that you Loved so much are now Gone," they will say as they Cry and Lament over her. "Yes, all of your Luxuries and your Great Splendor are gone Forever, never to be yours again: because you have Vanished in a Cloud of Radiation."

Y-[_] Yes, the Merchants who became Wealthy by Selling her those Things will Stand afar off at a Safe Distance, being Terrified by her Great Torment; and thus they will Weep and Cry Out: "How Terrible, how Awful it has been for that Great City! Yes, she was Clothed in the Finest of Purple and Scarlet Linens, being Decked out with Gold and Silver and Precious Stones and Countless Pearls around the Necks of the Ladies! But, in a single Moment of Time, all of the Wealth of that City of Confusion has Vanished!" And thus all of the Captains of the Merchant Ships and their Passengers and Sailors and Crews will Stand afar off at a Safe Distance. Yes, they will Cry Out as if in Agony as they Watch the Smoke of her Burning ascend into the Sky, and they will say: "Where is there another City as Great as this one was?" And thus they will Weep and Mourn and Throw Dust on their Heads to show their Great Grief and Sorrow over her. And they will Cry Out, "Alas, Alas, how Terrible, how Awful for that Great City! The Shipowners became Wealthy by Transporting her Goods and Great Wealth across the Seas; but, behold, in a single Moment of Time, it has all Vanished in a Great Cloud of Radioactive Dust!"

Z-[_] Rejoice over her Evil Fate, O you Angels of Heaven and People of God, even you Apostles and Holy Prophets: because at Last the God of Justice has Arisen from his Great Throne in the Sky, and has Rendered unto her True Justice for your Sakes! Yes, he has gotten Revenge for you on the Old Whore, who has made herself Rich with the Abundance of her Drugs for Sale. Then a Mighty Angel picked up a Boulder the Size of a Huge Millstone, being 20 feet in diameter, and he Threw it into the Ocean of Filthiness, and Shouted: "Just like this, that Great City of Confusion will be Thrown Down with Violence, and will never be Found again! Indeed, the Sound of Harps, Singers, Flutes, nor Trumpets will be Heard in you again. No Craftsmen nor Traders will ever be Found in you again; and the Sounds of the Mills will never be Heard in you again. The Light of a Lamp will never Shine in you again, nor the Happy Voices of Brides and Grooms will be Heard in you again: because you have come to your End: because your Merchants were the Greatest Sinners in the World: because you Deceived the Nations by the Abundance of your Druggeries. Moreover, in your Streets was Flowing the Blood of the Prophets and of God's Holy People, even the Blood of Innocent People, who were Slaughtered all over the World, shall be laid on you: because of your Greed and Selfishness, whereby you could never get Enough Money, even while your Bank Vaults were Full of Gold, while Multitudes of Poor People Starved to Death, and went down to their Graves with Grief, with Hunger and Thirst, while you Lived in Luxury with Drunken Gluttonous Fools."

11-11 [_] So, O Selected King, is that the End of the Sad Story? Is there no Happy Ending to it?

11-12 [_] Well, Chapter 19 goes on to say:

A-[_] After that, I Heard what Sounded like a Vast Multitude of Happy People in the Sky, shouting: "Praise the Supreme Ruler! Salvation and Glory and Power belong to our God, whose Judgments are True and Just. Yes, he has Punished the Old Whore, even the Mother of Prostitutes and the Producer of Abominations, who Corrupted the Whole Earth with her Immoralities. Therefore, God has Avenged the Murders of his Humble Servants."

B-[_] And again their Voices Rang Out throughout the World, saying: "Praise the Great Creator God, even the Supreme Ruler of Mankind! The Smoke and Stink from that Great City of Confusion Ascends Up forever and ever for a Memorial to her Wickedness!"

C-[_] Then the 24 Elders and the 4 Living Beings fell down and Worshiped God, who was sitting on the Throne in the Sky. Yes, they Cried Out, saying: "Amen! Praise the Supreme Ruler!" And from the Throne there came a Voice that said, "Praise our God, all of you who are his Servants, even all of you who Fear him who Created Lightning and Thunder, even from the Least Important among you to the Greatest among you."

D-[_] Then I Heard again what Sounded like the Shouting of a Vast Crowd of People, or perhaps the Roar of Mighty Ocean Waves, or the Crashing of Gideon's Pitchers on the Rocks, or the Clapping of Thunderbolts, saying: "Praise the Supreme Ruler! For the Ruler our God, the Almighty God, Reigns over all of the Earth. Therefore, let us be Glad and Rejoice, and let us give Honor and Praise to him: because the Time has Come for the Great Wedding of the Nations Celebration, and the Wedding Feast of the Lamb of God: because his Bride has made herself Ready for his Return by Means of much Fasting and Praying, whereby she has become Holy, even as he is Holy, and has Purified herself, even as he is Pure. Therefore, she has been Given the Finest of Pure White Linen to Wear: because she has been Found Worthy." Indeed, the Fine Linen Represents the Good Deeds of God's Holy People, who will be Wise and Build Beautiful Planned City States, called: **"GLORIOUS Swanky Hotels Castles and Fortresses,"** where they can Live in Peace, and Attend to the Better Things in Life, and Raise Up Holy Children, and Live like Adam and Eve in the Garden of Eden, even as People were Designed to Live; and thus Walk Humbly with their God.

E-[_] And the Angel said to me, "Write these Words: Blest are those Wise People, who are Invited to the Wedding Feast of the Lamb of God, who become Holy, even as he is Holy." And then he added this Thought: "These are True Words, which come from God, who alone can be Trusted."

F-[_] Then I fell down at his Feet to Worship him; but, as before, he said: "No, do not Worship me: because I am a Fellow Servant of God with you, even as you and your Brothers and Sisters are, who Testify about their Faith in Jesus Christ. Therefore, Worship God, only: because the Essence of Prophecies is to give a Clear-cut Witness for Jesus, who is the Lamb of God, who was Slain to take Away the Sins of the World, even the Sins of those Wise People who Believe in him, and Obey his Commandments, who shall Feast on the Sweet Fruits from the Tree of Life, Forever."

G-[_] Then I saw the Sky Open up again, and a White Horse was Standing there, being Dressed for Battle with Armor on, made of Polished Silver with Gold Trimmings; and his Rider was Named Faithful and True: because he Judges Fairly and Justly, and thus Wages a Righteous War against all of his Enemies with his Sharp Sword of Divine Truths. His Eyes were like the Blue Flames of a very Hot Fire, and on his Head were many Crowns of Glory. A Name was also written on him that no one Understood, except himself. He Wore a Robe that was Dipped in Blood, and his Title was "The Words of God in Person." Moreover, the Armies of Heaven were Dressed in the Finest of Pure White Linen, who Followed him on their White Horses, which were also Dressed for Battle.

H-[_] From his Mouth came forth a Sharp Sword to Strike Down the Nations of Rebellious ones, whereby he will Rule them with a Rod of Iron, which Represents the Words of God. Moreover, he will Release the Fierce Wrath of Almighty God, like Juice Flowing from a Winepress, whereby all Nations will be Squeezed in the Press. On his Robe at his Thigh, this Title was written: King of all Kings, and Ruler of all Rulers.

I-[_] Then I saw an Angel Standing in the Sun, Shouting to the Vultures who were Flying in the Sky, saying: "Come! Gather yourselves Together for the Great Feast that God has Prepared for you. Come and Eat the Flesh of Greedy Kings, Murderous Generals, and Strong Warriors; of Horses and their Riders, and all of Humanity, both Free and Slave, Small and Great, if they do not Humbly Submit to the Sword of Truths."

J-[_] Then I saw the Beast and the Kings of the World and their Armies, all Gathered Together to Fight Against the Holy One who was sitting on his White Horse, and his Great Army on their Horses. And the Beast was Captured, and with him the False Prophet, who did mighty Miracles on behalf of the Beast — even Manmade Miracles, whereby they Deceived all People who had Accepted the Mark of the Beast, and who Worshiped his Image that Speaks Lies and Deceptions, and Advertises Drugs and Horseless Wagons. Both the Beast and his False Prophet were Thrown Alive into the Fiery Lake of Burning Sulfur, which Smelled like Rotten Eggs. Indeed, their entire Army was Killed by the Sharp Sword of Provable Truths, which came out of the Mouth of the Holy One, who was Riding the Great White Horse. And the Vultures were Gorging themselves on the Dead Bodies, which were many.

K-[_] Then I saw an Angel coming down from the Sky with the Key to the Bottomless Pit in his Right Hand with a Heavy Chain in his Left Hand, who Seized the Dragon — even that Old Serpent, who Deceived Mother Eve, who is known as the Devil, even Satan, himself — and thus the Holy Angel Bound him in Chains for a Thousand Years. Yes, the Angel Threw him into the Bottomless Pit, and then he Shut the Trapdoor, and Locked Satan in it: so that he could not Deceive the Nations anymore, until the Thousand Years were Finished; and then he will be Released for a short Season, in Order to Test the People of the Nations one more Time, in Order for God to Discover whether or not the People have Learned their Lessons.

L-[_] Then I saw Thrones Set Up, and the People who were Sitting on them had been given the Authority to Judge the People. And I saw the Souls of those who had been Beheaded for their Testimonies about Jesus Christ, and for Proclaiming the Words of God. Moreover, they had not Worshiped the Beast, nor his Image that Speaks Lies, nor had they Accepted his Identification Mark on their Foreheads, nor in their Hands. Therefore, they all came back to Life again, being Born in New Bodies; and thus, when they Grew Up, they Reigned with Christ on the Earth for a Thousand Years.

M-[_] That is the First Resurrection; and the Remainder of the Dead People did not come back to Life, until the Thousand Years had Ended, at which Time they were Born here again, in Order to be Tested one more Time. Blest and Holy are those Wise People who Share in the First Resurrection: because, for them, the Second Death has no Power; but, they will be Priests, Teachers, Administrators, Rulers, Governors, and Kings of God and of Christ, and will Reign with him for a Thousand Years on the Earth: because of being found Worthy for their Occupations.

N-[_] Now, when the Thousand Years shall come to an End, Satan will be let Out of his Prison, in Order to go Out to Deceive the Nations one more Time — both Inside and Outside of the Earth, which is known as Gog and Magog — in every Corner of the Earth. Yes, he will Gather them Together for Battle, even a Mighty Army, being as Numberless as the Grains of Sand along the Seashore, you might say: because no one will be Able to Count them. However, I Heard the Number of them, and it was 200 Billion.

O-[_] And I saw them as they went up on the Broad Plain of the Earth, and Surrounded God's People in the Beloved City. But, Fire came down from the Sky on the Attacking Armies, and it Consumed them while they Stood on their Feets, whereby their Tongues were Consumed in their Mouths, and their Eyeballs Fell from their Sockets: because they would not Use their Eyes to Study the Works of Provable Truths, nor Use their Tongues to Speak those Truths; but, they found much Time for Foolishness, Sports and War Games.

P-[_] Then the Devil, who had Deceived them, was Thrown Alive into the Fiery Lake of Burning Sulfur, where he Joined the Beast and the False Prophet; and there they will be Tormented both Day and Night, forever and ever: because that is the Just Reward for those who go into Perdition. Indeed, they will take the Blame for all of the Evils that have been done on the Earth: beCause they Inspired all such Evils, while the People will be Judged According to their Words and Works: because they all had Choices to make, and some Chose to Say and Do Good Things, and others Chose to Say and Do Evil Things.

(HOW all People can Prosper in a RIIT WAA, and Stop Polluting the Earth with Capitalist TRASH!)

Q-[_] And then I saw a Great White Throne made of Ivory, and a Holy One was Sitting on it; and the People of the Earth, and the Angels of the Sky Fled from his Presence; but, they found no Place to Hide.

R-[_] So, I saw the Dead, both Great and Small, Standing in front of God's Throne; and the Books were Opened up, including this Book, and the Book of Life, also; and the Dead People were Judged According to whatever they had Said and Done, according to whatever was written in the Books, and Recorded in Court Houses, whereby all such Records might be Corrected According to the Records of the Holy Angels, who were also Keeping Records of the Facts and Actual Events, whereby nothing was kept Secret.

S-[_] The Seas also gave up their Dead People, even if they were nothing but Ashes; and the Angel of Death and the Grave gave up their Dead; and all were Judged According to their Words and Deeds during all of their Lives, no matter how many Times they Lived and Died and were Judged by God, and Sent to Appropriate Places for them to Learn their Lessons, and thus be Recycled again and again, until they are brought to Perfection for either Good or Evil, being Prepared for God's Holy Kingdom, or Satan's Unholy Kingdom.

T-[_] Then the Angels of Death and the Grave were Thrown into the Lake of Fire, which is the Second Death and Final Punishment. Moreover, anyone whose Name was not Found Recorded in the Book of Life was Thrown into the Lake of Fire with them: because they were not Found Worthy to Live, being Proven to be Unworthy.

U-[_] Then I saw a Renewed Heaven and a Renewed Earth: because the Old Heaven and the Old Earth had Disappeared, and there were no more Great Oceans; but, there were Lakes and Rivers and Small Seas Covering the New Earth, which was Designed for Great Multitudes of People to Live all around the Central Belt, which was at the Perfect Elevation for a Perfect Climate the Year around.

V-[_] And then I saw the Holy City of God, even a New Jerusalem, coming down from God Out of the Sky, like a Bride who is Beautifully Adorned for her Husband, which City Entered into the Hollow Earth, where there is no Night, nor Light from the Sunstar, nor any Deceptive Moon, which Symbolizes the Devil.

W-[_] Then I Heard a Loud Voice from the Throne, saying: "LOOK, God's Home is now among his People; and he will Live with them, and be their Supreme Ruler, and they will be his Humble and Obedient People. Yes, God, himself, will be with them, to Teach to them his Ways, and to Guide them in the Ways of Righteousness. Therefore, he will Wipe Away every Tear from their Eyes, and there will be no more Death, Sorrow, Crying, nor Pains: because all of those Former Things will be Gone Forever. Yes, the Masses of People will Learn the Whole Truth, whereby they will become Healthy, Wealthy, and Wise, and thus Live in Peace with one another."

X-[_] And the Holy One, who was sitting on the Throne, said: "Behold, I am making everything New!" And then he said to me, "Write this in a Book: because, what I tell you is Trustworthy and True."

Y-[_] And he also said, "It is Finished! I am the Alpha and the Omega — even the Beginning of the Creation of Jehovah God in this World, and the End of his Perfection. Therefore, to all People who are Thirsting for the Truth, I will Give Freely from the Living Springs of the Water of Life. Therefore, Drink Freely, and Satisfy your Souls with my Inspired Words of Provable Truths. All who are Victorious, and Overcome all of their Sins, and Stop Sinning, and Practice Fidelity, will Inherit all of these Blessings, and I will be their God, and they will be my Adopted Children. But, Spiritual Cowards, Unbelievers, Corrupted Politicians, Murderers, Immoral People, those who Practice Witchcraft, Idol Worshipers, Infidels, Whoremongers, Warmongers, Sodomites, and all Liars shall have their Places in the Lake of Fire with Burning Sulfur, which is the Second Death."

Z-[_] Then one of the Seven Angels, who held the Seven Bowls containing the Seven Last Great Plagues, came and said to me: "Come with me! I will now Show to you the Bride, even the Wife of the Lamb, which is his Holy Church." So, he took me by the Power of the Spirit to a Great High Mountain, and he Showed to me the Holy City, even the New Jerusalem, descending Out of the Sky from God. Indeed, it Shined with the Glory of God, and Sparkled like a Precious Gemstone — like an Amethyst, Sapphire or Emerald Stone, as clear as Crystal, set on a Foundation of Red Jasper and Blue Amber. The City Wall was very Broad and High, with 12 Gates, Guarded by 12 Holy Angels; and the Names of the 12 Tribes of Israel were written on the Gates. There were 3 Gates on each Side of the City, which was Square at the Base, and Shaped like the Great Pyramid in Egypt, being Equally as High as it was Wide and Long, being 1,400 Miles High, being made of Pure Gold on the Outside, being as Clear as Glass, from which the Light of God Shined and Lighted the Hollow Earth: because the City Rested in the Center of it on a Cloud. The Wall of the City had 12 Foundation Stones, and on them were written the Names of the 12 Apostles of the Lamb. The Wall that Surrounded the Holy City was also Built on Foundation Stones, being Inlaid with 12 Precious Stones all about: the first was Jasper, the second Sapphire, the third Agate, the fourth Emerald, the fifth Onyx, the sixth Carnelian, the seventh Chrysolite, the eighth Beryl, the ninth Topaz, the tenth Chrysoprase, the eleventh Jacinth, and the twelfth Amethyst. The 12 Gates were made of 12 Giant Pearls, whereby each Gate was one Pearl, being Rolled to one Side, which was not Closed at any Time. And the Main Street was Paved with Pure Gold, being as Clear as Glass, which Street ran from one Side of the City in a Ziggurat, around and around the City, until it reached the Top of it, where the Throne of God was Set Up, from which Poured Forth the River of Life, which ran Down from the Top to the Bottom of the City, in the Middle of the Golden Street, having the Trees of Life Bordering the River on each Side, being Bordered by the Golden Street on each Side, which was Bordered with Beautiful Palaces on each Side, all along the Street, from Terrace to Terrace, having Beautiful Stone Dome Homes within the Terraces, which Rested on Huge Cisterns at the Bottom, where the Water was Stored, until it was Pumped Up to the Great Throne. Indeed, the Riverbed was Filled with Polished Jasper and Granite Boulders of Various Sizes and Colors: so that the Water was Purified as it ran down to the Cisterns, which was used for Watering all of the Beautiful Gardens. However, I saw no Temple in the City: because the Supreme Ruling God Almighty and the Lamb are the Temple. And the City has no Need of the Sun nor Moon: because the Glory of God Illuminates it, and the Lamb is its Light, himself. Moreover, the Nations will Walk in its Light all around within the Hollow Earth; and the Holy Kings of the World will Enter the City in all of their Glory. Indeed, its Gates will never be Closed at the End of Day: because there is no Night

(HOW all People can Prosper in a RIIT WAA, and Stop Polluting the Earth with Capitalist TRASH!)

there, nor does anyone get Tired enough to Sleep for more than a few Minutes at a Time; and all of the Nations will bring their Glory and Honor into the Holy City; but, nothing Evil will be Allowed to Enter, nor anyone who Practices Shameful Things — such as Gluttony, Drunkenness, Idolatry, Adultery, Sodomy, Druggery, and Dishonesty — but, only those People whose Names are found Written in the Lamb's Book of Life. And thus the Great Pyramid Government of God will be Established, whereby the Apostles and Holy Prophets and Patriarchs will be Established at the Top of the Pyramid, near to the Throne of God, himself, who is a Giant of a Man, being no less than 400 feet Tall!

11-13 [_] So, O Selected King, does God have a Sense of Humor, or what? Such a City would be Out of the Atmosphere! Therefore, it is just Ridiculous. †§‡

11-14 [_] Well, the City is Enclosed by the Golden / Glass Pyramid, and it has its own Atmosphere within each Story; and there are no less than 1,200 Stories: because each Story is more than a Mile High, and is Designed like a Ziggurat on the Outside, so that the single River of Water runs down from the Top, and Waters the entire City, which is a Great River, which Branches Out to the Gardens as it comes Flowing Down at a Gentle Grade from the Throne Room at the Top. In other Words, it is a Mile or more Wide at the Top, which has a Great Waterfalls at the Head of it, about 5 Miles from the Great Throne with the Sea of Glass in front of it, where a hundred-million People can Stand at one Time.

11-15 [_] O Selected King, how many Years would it Require for a Person to Walk up to the Great Throne Room from one of the Pearly White Gates at the Bottom?

11-16 [_] Well, if a Person were to Follow the Golden Street of the Ziggurat, around and around on each Story, and the First Story is 1,200 Miles on just one Side, and an Average of 600 Miles on each Story, all of the Way to the Top, having an Average of 2,400 Miles on just one Step or Terrace of the Ziggurat of each Story, or a Total of an Average of 2,400 Miles on the Street of each Story, Times 1,200 Stories, we are talking about 2,880,000 Miles of Highway to Walk Up! Therefore, if we should Stop to take a Look at each Unique Stone Dome Home along that Great Street that is Paved with Pure Gold, and also Stop to take a Good Look at each Beautiful Garden, and on each Story, all of the way around it a hundred Times or more, I would say that it would Require no less than a Million Years to get from the Bottom of the City to the Top of it — Depending on what Interesting People that we might Meet on the Way Up to the Throne: beCause of having no less than 100 Billion People in there to Meet! After all, there are Gardens on the Roofs of all of the Stone Dome Homes, which are Watered by the River of Life, which Flows Down from the Throne, and Runs Around the Ziggurat within each Story, each of which is like a Great Pyramid or Ziggurat Pyramid with Tunnels and Elevators throughout each Floor, with Electric Subway Trains for Transportation within each Great Story, which has no less than 70 Terraces within each Ziggurat Terrace for each Story. Therefore, even if you Bypassed all of those Billions of Stone Dome Homes, and went from one Elevator to another one, until you got to the Top, it would still Require a Month or more of Time to get from the Bottom to the Top of the Great Holy City: beCause there are no less than 84,000 Elevators! However, no one in his or her Right Mind would Want to Pass by all of those Marblelous Stone Dome Homes, even at the Bottom Level of the City: beCause of their Exquisite Beauty, being made Perfect by the Holy Angels who Built them, according to the Instructions of the Master Farmer at the Top, who, of course, has the most Beautiful Stone Dome Homes near to his Throne, where Multitudes of Giants Live: beCause the largest Giants are at the

Top, who get smaller and smaller as one comes Down from the Top; or, who get larger and larger as one goes Up from the Bottom: because the People and their Homes get larger and LARGER as one goes Up, until at last one comes to the Great Throne Room, itself, which is no less than 10 Miles Wide, just to Accommodate that Great Sea of Glass and 100,000,000 People!

11-17 [_] So, O Selected King, in Order for God to be Seen on his Throne from such a Great Distance, it is Necessary for him to be a Great GIANT, huh?

11-18 [_] Yes, that is the Truth of it. Otherwise, he would be Invisible from 5 Miles Away; but, being a Great Giant, about 400 Feet Tall, he can be Seen Sitting on his Great Golden Throne, Laden with Gemstones, even from 5 Miles Away.

11-19 [_] So, O Selected King, does Almighty God have Telescopic Eyeballs, whereby he can See those Tiny People, who are 5 Miles Away from him on the Sea of Glass?

11-20 [_] Well, of course he has very Good Eyesight, and can See Clearly for a hundred Miles Away. Therefore, that is no Problem. Moreover, everything about him is Gigantic, including his Voice, whereby he will not Need a Megaphone to Talk to everyone on that Sea of Glass, which Throne Room has Perfect Acoustics, even if he is Whispering, whereby everyone will be Able to Hear him Perfectly: beCause of the Design of the Room.

11-21 [_] O Selected King, can you Visualize what such a Naked Giant would Look Like? Indeed, if he should Ejaculate his Sperm, it would Fill a 50-gallon Barrel, and would Shoot Out no less than 1,000 Feet from him, and Especially if he has never had Sex in a Million Years or so! After all, according to Saint Peter, a thousand Years is one Day to God. †§‡ (See *2 Peter 3:8*.)

11-22 [_] Well, there is no Mention of his Wife. Therefore, it could be that he has never had any Sex. However, I am Curious to Learn just how much he might Eat at one Meal, since a Bushel of Apples would only be one Bite with a Big Spoon. Moreover, if he were a Body Builder, he would certainly have some Large Beautiful Muscles, which would be in Perfect Proportion to his Size. After all, he would Naturally have the most Perfect Body of any Creature, which would give new Meaning to the Phrase: *"For Thine is the Kingdom, the Power, and the Glory, Forever. Amen."* — *Matthew 6:13, RKJV*.

11-23 [_] O Selected King, do you Actually Believe all such Religious Nonsense? §

11-24 [_] Well, if those Pearly White Gates are each made of just ONE Pearl, we would have to Confess that such Pearls came from GIANT Pearl Oyster, perhaps as Tall as the Empire State Building in New York City! Therefore, in such a Marvelous Universe, anything is Possible, including the GIANTS. Therefore, why should I not Believe it? Just Think about those Giant Nebulas, which can be tens of Trillions of Light-years across them, wherein Giant Stars are being Born on a Regular Basis, which might be a Trillion Times as Big as our Tiny Sunstar! Therefore, we can Honestly say that God is a Great Giant, who is in the Business of Creating more and more GIANTS! But, for Sure, there are enough Stars in the Universe for each Human Being on this Earth to Inherit at least a Billion of them, each!

(HOW all People can Prosper in a RIIT WAA, and Stop Polluting the Earth with Capitalist TRASH!)

— Chapter 12 —

An Explanation of the Cover Photo

12-01 [_] O Selected King, I am Glad that you have now come back down to the Earth: because, when you are Traveling in the Spirit into other Worlds, it is a little Weird to us, and Unrealistic. For Example, HOW could there be a Holy City that is 1,400 Miles Tall, and Equally as Wide and Long, with 100 Billion People Living in it? Can you begin to Imagine how STRONG those Surrounding Glass Walls would have to be, just to Support the Windows? Moreover, each Ziggurat Floor or Story would have to be Supported with Granite Stones a quarter of a Mile THICK, in Great Arches, which would have to Rest on something other than Atmosphere. †§‡

12-02 [_] Well, each Great Floor of the Ziggurat is Resting on Great Granite Pillars all around it on the Outside, on the Inside of the Glass "Windows," which are also very THICK and Self-supporting, which also have Tunnels within them for People to Walk through, and Look Out of Windows at the Surrounding Hollow Earth, which is the Paradise, which is Covered with 10 Times as much Land as we have on the Outside of the Earth: beCause the "Crust" of the Earth is only about 1,000 Miles Thick, which Means that the Inside of the Hollow Earth is about 6,000 Miles in Diameter, and has only Small Lakes and Rivers: so that most of it is LAND, which is Inhabited by hundreds of Billions of People, many of which are GIANTS! Yes, some of them are 36 Feet Tall, who Naturally have LARGE Houses with Tall Doorways and BIG Rooms, the likes of which only Giants could Build! †‡

12-03 [_] So, O Selected King, it Sounds as if we are the Barbarians on the Outside of the Earth! Do those Giants Eat a whole Cow at one Meal, or three 200-pound Pigs and 40 Chickens?

12-04 [_] Well, they have Giant Fruits to Eat — such as 200-pound Watermelons, which are very Sweet and Delicious, which you can Dream about, if you are Close to God, whereby you might get a Glimpse of Things to Come.

12-05 [_] O Selected King, I Think that you have been Using some Exotic Drugs, whereby you have had Hallucinations about Things that are Unreal. Therefore, tell us about your Retirement Home in Mexico: because we might be able to Relate with it.

12-06 [_] Well, as you can See in the Photo on Page 3, the Pillars or Columns are 2-feet by 2-feet thick, and 9 feet tall, and the Solid Concrete Walls (both Interior and Exterior) are 8-inches thick, which is NOT Normal for any House, even in Mexico. However, there are lots of Ancient Buildings in Mexico, which have much Thicker Stone Walls — such as those at Uxmal (pronounced Qsh-mawl in Funetik Ingglish), for which you can see many Photos in *Wikipedia;* but, not nearly ALL of the Buildings that are there: because it was a Great City, which was probably Inhabited by a Million or more People. Notice that the Great Pyramid at Uxmal is not Presently Covered with Pure Gold, as it once was, according to the Angel, who Talked with me in my Dream. The Gold was Robbed when the City was Abandoned. Nevertheless, at the Height of its Glory, it was a very Great City. †‡

12-07 [_] O Selected King, it seems that Ancient Societies were far Advanced over Present Societies, huh?

12-08 [_] Well, it Silently Testifies to the Great Advantages of SWANGKEENOMIKS! Indeed, it Proves that Great Things can be Accomplished by a Superior Economic System, which I call Swangkeenomiks, which makes all such Good Things Possible. In Fact, it is otherwise known as "United Effort with Unlimited Natural Resources and Money." Yes, without a Righteous One-World Government, it is Impossible for the Masses of People to Prosper as they should, and as they would, and as they will when the Masses of People come to their Riit Sensuz, and Elect me to be their Riichus King! {See www.Amazon.com for: **"Mark Twain Races for the PRESIDENCY!" (The 2020 Presidential Candidates Desperately Need Some STRONG Undefeatable COMPETITION!)**, Book 033, plus: **"Does a Good Soldier have to be a MURDERER?" (Seven Great Swanky Armies of Voluntary Working Soldiers!)**, Book 027, plus: **"A Sound Argument for Masters and Servants!" (WHY Everyone Needs a Good Master, and every Master Needs Good Obedient Servants!)**, Book 008, plus: **"God Speaks and the Whole World Listens!" (Fire on the Mountain from the Burning Bush by the Spirit of Truth!)**, Book 026, plus: **"The Right Design for Living!" (A List of Great Advantages for Building Beautiful Planned City States!)**, Book 012, plus: **"The Environmentalists' Paradise!" (HOW almost Everyone could be Living in a Beautiful Manmade Paradise!)**, Book 035, plus: **"UNLIMITED ENERJEE 99 Percent Pollutions Free!" (HOW to Obtain FREE ElecTrickery, Worldwide!) By The Worldwide People's Revolution!®** Book 029.}

12-09 [_] So, O Selected King, just how many Rooms and Walls are there in your Retirement Home?

12-10 [_] Well, all of that is Explained in: **"What is WRong with those Professing Christians?" (A Self-Examination of the Heart of the Body of Good Government!) By The Worldwide People's Revolution!®,** Book 002, which has a Photo of the Front of the House on the Cover, with the Unfinished Porch. However, you can see many Photographs with Explanations in: **"What is WRong with those CRAZY Christians?" (A Self-Examination of the Heart of the Body of Good Government!)**, Book 076, which is a Companion Book of the above Book. {FOOTNOTE: At the Time when I wrote Book 002, I did not know how to Insert the Photos into it, which turned out to be a Good Thing: beCause Book 002 Costs much less than Book 076, with all of its Colored Photos, which most People cannot Afford. But, Collectively, they could Afford all of them.} The Cover Photo for this Book is Self-Explanatory. It is a Trash Truck being Filled with more Trash for the Trash Dump. There are millions of such Trucks in this World of Woes, and much of that Trash ends up in the Oceans, Seas, Lakes, Rivers, and Forests. Some States Charge their People to take their Trash to a Dump, which Encourages them to Dump it in the Forests. Some Chemical Companies haul Tanker Truckloads of Toxic Liquid Wastes into National Forest Preserves to Dump it, rather than Pay to have it Disposed of "Properly" at some Government Waste Dump. That way they Save Money, in spite of getting Fined if they get Caught: because they might make several hundred Illegal Dumps before getting Caught. I have Caught them, myself, in Arkansas, and Reported them; but, nothing was Done about it. Perhaps the EPA (Environmental Protection Agency) was being Paid some "Look-away Money" for Ignoring it. The Swamp in Washington has Long Tentacles, you might say, which reach out from Coast to Coast. I have also seen Used Motor Oil being Dumped in Toilets in Arkansas Automotive Repair Garages, to "Save the Environment by the Republican Plan." And they even Professed to be "Christians." †§‡§§

(HOW all People can Prosper in a RIIT WAA, and Stop Polluting the Earth with Capitalist TRASH!)

— Chapter 13 —

Is Swangkeenomiks the Best Way to Exercise our Faith in God?

13-01 [_] Well, it is for Sure that Capitalism is NOT the Best Way to Exercise our Faith in God: beCause it has Produced X-amount of High-ranking Criminals, and Multitudes of Low-ranking Criminals, some of whom are now in All-American Prisons. In Fact, when a whole City RIOTS, it can be Burned Down by those "Good Capitalists," who also often LOOT the Stores, Break Out Expensive Windows, and otherwise Cause a LOT of Damage, which often adds up to Millions of Dollars, even for "Minor Incidents" — as a Result of Capitalistic Construction Plans, such as Tornadoes passing by All-American Trashy Houses, while Kissing them Goodbye, which would be of little Concern to those Wise People, who have Constructed those **"GLORIOUS Swanky Hotels Castle and Fortresses!"** Therefore, even some Forms of Communism has Proven to be Better than Capitalism: beCause Crime went Up in Russia by 7,000% when Capitalism was Adopted by the Russians, and Communism was put to Rest with Saint Joseph Stalin and Vladimir Ilich Lenin, who was by far the Better one of the 2 Criminals; but, he was not nearly as Good as Adolf Hitler, who will Certainly Enter into the Kingdom of God before those MEAN Communists. Remember that German Soldiers did not Rape any Russian Women when they Invaded Russia, while Communist Russians Raped tens of thousands of German Women when they Invaded. †§‡

13-02 [_] O Selected King, have you Lost your Riit Miind? The Dictator, Adolf Hitler, was a thousand Times WORSE than Saint Joseph Stalin! †§‡

13-03 [_] Can you Prove that in a Courtroom? I Believe that Joseph Stalin was a thousand Times more Evil than Adolf, and I can Prove it in a Courtroom. In Fact, I have already Proven it within my Inspired Books, if you care to Study them. Moreover, the Reason WHY Adolf Hitler was so "BAD," was beCause his Enemies wrote the History Books that tell about him, which are mostly Propagandist LIES: beCause the History Books Favor the Edomite Bankers, while Discrediting Adolf Hitler as some Kind of a Raving MANIAC! In Fact, you would only have to Watch a few Red Jew Movies about Hitler, which Repeatedly show him "on Stage" within the middle of some HOT Speech, where he is Acting like a Real Orator of his Caliber should, just to Work Up an Appetite for what he was Proposing, which made Good Sense to most of the Germans. In Fact, 95% or more of the Germans LOVED Adolf Hitler, whereby he could Freely Ride around in Open Cars on the Streets, while American Presidents have to have Armored Cars and 5,000+ Security Guards, while Adolf Hitler only needed 2, to Watch behind his Back for some Lying Murderous Red Jew of the Bernie Madoff and Judas Iscariot Club. After all, in Germany at that Time, if someone Objected to the Ideas of Adolf Hitler, they could Present their most Reasonable Arguments at their Meetings of the Minds, whereby their Questions could be Answered by People who knew what they were Talking about, which you cannot Do in **"The Divided States of United Lies!"** Indeed, just Try to get into the Democratic National Convention (DNC) with a Republican Question; or, just Try to get into the Republican National Convention with a Democratic Question, and see how far you get! In Fact, that is the very Reason that those Phony Parties Install 12-feet-high Fences with Concertinaed Wire at the Top of the Fences, just to Protect those Phony

Politicians, while President Abraham Lincoln was not at all Afraid to Face his Opponents, Man to Man, and Answer any Important Questions like a Man should. Indeed, if he did not know the Answer to something, he was Man enough to Admit it, while these Modern Politicians Evade the Subjects, and normally never Confess their Ignorance about anything. †§‡

13-04 [_] O Selected King, if Adolf Hitler was such a GOOD Guy, how come he Lost the War? Is God not always on the Side of the Good Guys, as in the Case of the Crucifixion of Jesus Christ, whereby Blood-thirsty Red Jews had him Crucified, while they got by with Murder? †§‡§§

13-05 [_] How come General Robert E. Lee Lost the Civil War? Can any Honest Person Rightly Deny that Robert E. Lee was by FAR more Righteous than Ulysses S. Grant, who was another one of those Cigar-chomping Whiskey-drinking Foul-mouthed Drunkards of the Selfish Capitalist Kind, who did not Object to Losing twice as many Men as the South Lost: beCause that is the Nature of PIGS, who only Care about themselves, who do not Mind Sacrificing X-amount of Soldiers: because they are like Cannon Fodder to them, who are Expendable, like Used Toilet Paper! Otherwise, there would not have been any Normandy Invasion during World War 2: beCause Adolf Hitler — like him or not — Invited American, British, and French Officials to have a Meeting of the Minds and an International Radio Debate over the Issues of the Time, rather than go to War; but, American and British Officials REFUSED to MEET with him: beCause they Knew for a Fact that they were in the WRong! Indeed, if the Sword of Truth had been on their Side, they would not have been Afraid to MEET, and in Front of all TV Cameras and Radio Microphones. However, being Spiritual COWARDS, they Refused to TALK, even as President George Warmonger Bush Refused to Talk with Saddam Hussein before Bombing Innocent People in Iraq, which is Documented by CBS News with Dan Rather, who had a Personal Interview with Saddam Hussein in Iraq. Therefore, rather than Talk about it, they Forced Adolf to take Action, which he did. However, he was Bucking Up Against both Capitalists and Communists, who comprised about 95% of the World, who also had 95% of the World's Natural Resources to Work with, while Adolf did not even have Motor Oil, nor Gasoline that was Exploited in Germany, which is still Importing Fuel from Russia. Therefore, he should have Accepted the Good Advice of Jesus Christ, and first sat down to Count the Cost, in Order to Know whether or not he could take on the Legions of the Synagogue of Satan with only 5% as many Soldiers! Amazingly enough, he almost Won: beCause those Highly-Educated Germans just Happened to have Superior Technologies at that Time, and were much Better Warriors by 10 Times. For Example, in the Battle of Monte Cassino, in Italy, the Allies Lost 55,000+ Troops with many more thousands Wounded, while the Germans Lost about 2,000 Troops with 18,000 Wounded. Moreover, the Heroic / Cowardly Americans Dropped 1,400 TONS of Bombs on the Abbey, and did not Kill even one German: beCause the German Troops were not IN the Abbey! Yes, it was a Miscalculation by Americans, who Sorely Lost all of the Way Around: beCause they were Fighting for an Anti-Christ Capitalist System that was Inspired by Satan, even as I have Proven in: **"The Nature of CAPITALISM!" (A List of the EVILS of CAPITALISM!) By The Worldwide People's Revolution!® Book 038.** †‡

13-06 [_] O Elected King, are you Suggesting that ALL Americans are COWARDS, just because of Dropping Cowardly Atomic Bombs on Japan? Was that not the Wisdom of GOD, who Inspired the Atomic Bomb, in Order to Protect his Chosen People — such as Albert Einstein, Robert Oppenheimer, Edward Teller, Alan Greenspan, Larry Silverstein, Henry Kissinger, and many Jewish Saints — such as Benjamin Netanyahu and Shitshak Rabeen? †§‡§§

(HOW all People can Prosper in a RIIT WAA, and Stop Polluting the Earth with Capitalist TRASH!)

13-07 [_] Well, if they were such Honorable and Trustworthy People, how come they do not Want to Attend: **"The GREAT Worldwide TELEVISED Court HEARING!"**? Are they not near Relatives of George Warmonger Bush and Little Dick Chicanery, Incorporated, who also have no Interest in Attending any such Great Meetings of the Most Intelligent Minds? Indeed, if they were not all Spiritual COWARDS, they would be Happy to take up their Swords of Truths and Defend themselves. However, the Truth is, they are all COWARDS, who are Afraid of a Courtroom, while I am NOT: beCause I Know for a Fact that the Truth is on MY SIDE! Otherwise, I would get some E-mail Letters for my **"FREEDUM uv SPEECH!" (A Special Magazine of Honest Opinions!) By The Worldwide People's Revolution!®**, Book 030-0002. †‡

13-08 [_] O Selected King, if you Imagine that you can Rightly Defend Adolf Hitler, you are NUTS: beCause he was the Chief Manager of the Jewish HOLOCAUST! †§‡

13-09 [_] Well, I See that you have Failed to do your "Homework," as they say. Indeed, there are many YouTube Videos on the Internet that DEBUNK the HoloHOAX, just in Case you have not been Informed about the TRUTH of it. However, Disregarding those hundreds of Videos, you are Welcome to Visit the HoloHOAX Museum in the District of Criminals, in Washington, and Check Out the Red Jew LIES for yourself, and take Photographs of all such Lies — except that Photographs are Forbidden by those Lying Red Jews: beCause they are Worse than the NAZIS! Indeed, they do not Want anyone to Question anything within those "Sacred and Hallowed Walls." Nevertheless, I Challenge you to take a Good Look in there, and make some Notes in a Notebook for Evidence, since Photographs are not Allowed. Yes, just write down the Exact Words that are Posted on Placards — such as: "The Nazis put 4 to 5 bodies into one oven every 10 minutes," whereby they Cremated no less than "… 1,000 bodies per day." Imagine that, if you can! A Train comes into Auschwitz, Poland, with 2,000 Jews onboard, once per Week, and the Women and Children are Separated from the Men, who are sent off to Work Sites, while the Women and Children are conveniently rounded up and ushered into a single "Gas Chamber," where a thousand of them are Murdered during the middle of a Hot Summer, in August, and it is your Duty to get all of them Dragged Out of the Gas Chamber, which barely has Standing Room for only 100 People; and then you must Cremate them in 10 Ovens during that same Day! Yes, the Ovens are Cold, according to "Eyewitnesses," themselves, who have Reported that Fact in MILLIONS of Jewish books. Therefore, you must Heat Up those 10 Ovens with COAL for one whole Hour or more, just to get them Ready for the Dead Bodies; and then you Discover to your Amazement that only ONE Body can be Fitted through the Doorway of an Oven, instead of 4 or 5 Bodies, as you Learned in the Non-historic Holocaust Museum in George Washington's Backyard, which had NO Facts Checkers' Approvals. Yes, you Discover that a FAT Body is also Difficult to get through the Doorway: beCause it is only 18 to 19 inches Wide, and the Body must Ride on a Steel Table / Gurney / Stretcher, just to get put into the very HOT Oven, lest you should Cook yourself at 1000 °F; and then, after you finally get that Fat Lady Stuffed into the Oven, it Require no less than 4 to 8 HOURS to get her Cremated: beCause TEETH are very HARD Things to Burn Up, as well as those Bones, which you can Prove for yourself in your own Backyard, just by Attempting to Burn Up a Hog's Head, which you can Buy at the Local Butcher Shop. Indeed, a little Practical Experiment will do your Soul much Good, whereby you can Speak with a little more Authority — except that the Fire in your Backyard is not Hot Enough to Cremate the Hog's Head; but, the Crematory Oven at 4000 °F is Hot Enough. However, even at those very HIGH Temperatures, it still Requires 4 to 8 Hours, or more, to Cremate ONE Adult Male Body; and then it Requires at least another Hour to COOL OFF that HOT Oven, lest it should FRY your Eyeballs when you

Open the Door, and even MELT your Goggles to your Face: beCause such a Hot Oven is very DANGEROUS, which you might have Discovered by a Hot Oven in a Cook Stove, at only 500 °F, whereby you got yourself Burned, just by Touching it for a Split Second. Therefore, Imagine Standing in front of a very HOT Crematory Oven, and some Nazi Soldier is Poking you in the Ribs with his Bayonet, saying: "I Want you to get at least 4 Dead Bodies into that Oven every 10 Minutes, or else I will Stuff YOU into it!" Yes, that is what those Lying Red Jews would have you to Believe; but, it is FAR from the Truth about what Actually Happened! Indeed, the Oven Requires no less than one whole Hour to Cool Off enough to Safely Open the Door; and even then, everything must be Handled with THICK Insulated Fireproof Gloves and Special Tools, just for Removing the Steel Gurney from the Hot Oven, which is RED HOT, which will also Severely BURN YOU, if you Accidentally Touch it, whereby you would Scream "Bloody Murder," as they say, whereby that Nazi Soldier would Poke you in the Ass with his Bayonet, and say: "I will only give to you one more Chance to make a Stupid Mistake like that, and then I will put you into the Oven while still Alive, after Castrating you with a Chainsaw or Meat Cleaver!" So, with much Shaking and Trembling and Frustration, you Attempt to TIE 4 Dead Bodies onto the HOT Steel Gurney with Barbed Wires: beCause Slippery Naked Dead Bodies do not Stack Up very Well, nor Kindly Stay in the Positions that you leave them, which you would have Discovered, if you had been in World War 2! So, after farting around for an Hour, trying to Tie those Dead Bodies to the Gurney, while Avoiding the HOT Steel, and without any THICK Insulated Fireproof Gloves: beCause of the Stinginess of those Mean Nazis, you and some other Prisoner do Manage to get the Bodies Wired to the Gurney, only to Discover that the Doorway of the Oven is not half Big enough. Therefore, that Nazi Soldier, who is Standing just over your Shoulder with a Snarl on his Face, says: "I told you that I Want 4 or 5 Bodies on the Gurney every 10 Minutes, you damned idiot! Therefore, WHY have you not Obeyed me?" And you say, "God have Mercy on me — I Tried to Obey you; but, it did not Work, Sir." And he says, "Strip Off your Rags, and let me get my Knife out" — at which Time you are Shaking and Trembling so Badly that you cannot even Unzip your Pants! Therefore, the Soldier Plunges his Bayonet into your Guts, and throws you onto the Gurney, himself, and says: "Did I not Warn you? Why did you not OBEY me?" And with your Last Dying Breath, you say: "Sir, are you so Stupid that you could not See that not even 3 Bodies could be Fitted through that Doorway on the Oven?" And he Answers, "It was Stupid Germans like me who Kicked American Asses at Monte Cassino! Now, haul out that Scrotum and Tally Whacker!" And you say, "Sir, I cannot find them!" Yes, you are Scared half to Death, and Frying on Top of that Hot Gurney; but, a little Voice from Heaven says: "Fear not, my Son, in a Short Time you will be with me in Paradise: because, of such Holy People as you, the Kingdom of God is Constructed." And you say, "O Lord, what shall I Do?" And the Nazi Soldier says, "What shall you Do? Unzip those Pants!" Meanwhile, your Back and Legs have been COOKED on that Hot Gurney, and the entire Room is Filled with the Smoke and Stink of Burned Flesh; but, no one except you Notices it: beCause it is Routine, since all of the Bodies that were Tied to the Gurneys were Burning while more Bodies were being Tied to them! Indeed, there is no Way around it: beCause it would Require no less than 9 Minutes to Tie 4 Bodies to one Gurney with the Barbed Wires, even if you had Good Gloves on and 6 other Prisoners of War to Help you, which would leave you with just ONE Minute to get those Bodies Cremated! Yes, it might Work much Better, if you just had a HOT Barbecue Grill to put them on. †§‡§§

13-10 [_] I Swear to God, O Selected King, that there is not a more Disrespectful Person on the Surface of this Whole Earth, than YOU! Whatever Happened with your EMPATHY for those Poor Lying Red Jews? Can you not at least Sympathize with them? After all, 60 Million of them DIED during World War 2, and another 120 Million Barely Survived: beCause their Legs were Cut Off for Feeding the German Hogs! Yes, there was a Great Shortage of Food at that Time: beCause Americans had BOMBED the German Railways and Bridges, whereby the Trains were Useless; and therefore, the only Food that was left for Feeding the Hogs was the Legs of Jews, which were Amputated at their Hips! Yes, you can read all about it in the HoloHOAX Museum in Washington, District of Colombian Drug Addicts, who show a Pile of a hundred Pairs of Shoes, and then ask us to Believe that those are the Shoes of 6 Million Jews, without even Informing us that when Prisoners were brought into German Concentration Camps, including Auschwitz, they were Issued NEW Clothing, including NEW Shoes, NEW Eye Glasses, and whatever they Needed: beCause it was a WORK Camp, which had 5 Hospital Wards, and no less than 20,000 Record Books, and even an Office for the International Red Cross, which kept Track of every single Death, and Recorded all such Deaths in their own Record Books, which, when added up at the End of the War, amounted to a Total of less than 190,000 People from ALL Concentration Camps in Europe! Yes, that is the Official Report, which any Dimwitcrat or Reprobate can Discover for him or herself on the Internet. Just Search in YouTube for HOLOHOAX, and see what comes up. Indeed, there is only ONE Way to Solve that Dispute, and that is for the Masses of People to DEMAND "**The GREAT Worldwide TELEVISED Court HEARING!**" †§‡§§

13-11 [_] O Selected King, every Time that I see more than one Page without a New Paragraph within any of your Inspired Books, I Know for a Fact that I am about to Read something most Interesting: beCause, when you get Warmed Up and Excited over something, there is no one on this Earth who can begin to Compete with you for Extreme Sarcasms. However, I am Wondering if that Nazi Soldier finally Castrated that Lying Red Jew, who Reported all such Lies in his Anti-Nazi book, and published it Worldwide?

13-12 [_] Well, when we Hold those Great Meetings of the Most Intelligent Minds, we will Gather Up all of those Anti-Nazi Books, and Prove them to be True or False; and, if we Discover Lies in them, we will have them Edited Out, if those Books are Worth Saving; or otherwise, we will have them Sent to the Crematory for making ElecTrickery. Indeed, we will Clean Out the Public LIE-braries, unless someone can Prove that all such Books have some VALUE: beCause Swangkeenomiks Demands HONESTY. Indeed, there is no Way that People can Prosper if they are nothing but Thieves, Liars, Robbers, and Criminals like those Edomite Banksters. †‡

— Chapter 14 —

Does Swangkeenomiks Demand HONESTY?

14-01 [_] O Selected King of **The Worldwide People's Revolution!®**, if we got Rid of all of the LIES in the Public Schools and LIE-braries, what would be left to Read? Indeed, not even the *Holy Bible* would Pass that Test, and it has been around for thousands of Years! †§‡

14-02 [_] Well, being such a Good Book, we will have to Edit OUT any Provable Lies, and thus make it into a Trustworthy Book, which is True of all History Books, which should be Cleaned Up, along with *Wickedpedia,* which does not tell the Whole Truth about a LOT of Important Subjects, including the HoloHOAX, the Moon Landings, the Kennedy Assassination, nor what Actually Happened during September 11th, 2001. Indeed, their Articles are Obviously written mostly by Jews — that is, by Honest White Jews and Lying Red Jews. In Fact, if it were not so, you might even find an Article about me in *Wikipedia.* After all, I am the Premier Author in the Whole World, who holds several World Records as an Inspired Author! †§‡

14-03 [_] O Selected King, if you are the Premier Author in the Whole World, we are in for BIG Troubles: beCause you are not even a Scientist, much less a GENIUS like Albert Einstein, who used Mathematics to Prove that Space BENDS and Causes a "Time Warp," whereby Things are not as they Appear to be. For Example, it Appears that the Stars are Racing around the Earth every 24 Hours or so; but, in Reality, the Earth is merely Spinning on its Axis at about 1,040 Miles per Hour (MpH) at the Equator, while Spinning at about 100 MpH in Juno, Alaska, which Means that there would be a HUGE Amount of Centrifugal FORCE on the Great Pyramid in Egypt: beCause of the SPEED of the Earth at the Equator, while there would hardly be any Centrifugal Force at the North Pole, around the Imaginary Axle. Indeed, you can Discover the POWER of Centrifugal Force, just by putting a 20-pound Rock in a Bucket, and then Tie a 20-feet-long Rope to the Bail of that Bucket, and then SWING the Bucket around and around your Body by Means of the Rope, which will become more and more Difficult as the Bucket gets going Faster and FASTER! In Fact, the Centrifugal FORCE will become so Great that you can barely hang onto the Rope, if the Bucket is going Fast Enough: beCause the Bucket and Rock will Want to FLY AWAY. However, no matter how Fast you might Swing the Bucket, you will never get it going 1,040 MpH! In Fact, you will do Well to get it going 20 MpH with a 10-pound Rock in the Bucket. Therefore, just Try to Imagine the Great FORCE that would be Exerted on the Great Pyramid in Egypt, if it were Traveling at 1,030 MpH! Trust me, the "Ropes" of the Earth could not Keep it from FLYING AWAY! Therefore, if Scientists are Correct — that the Earth is Spinning on an Imaginary Axle or Axis at about 1,040 MpH — then there is no Way that *Joshua* could have Stopped the Earth from Spinning, so as to Finish his Battle in Chapter 10. †§‡

14-04 [_] Well, that is beCause Joshua Actually Stopped the SUN and Moon from Racing around the Earth, which never Moved an Inch! Indeed, if he had Stopped the Earth from Spinning, it would have Flung him and those Philistines into Heaven! Moreover, the Weightiness of the Great Pyramid would have also Caused it to become a Spaceship, like the Saturn V Rocket, which was Used Wisely for the Fake Moon Landings by the AstroNOTS, who barely got 25 Miles from the Earth, which is a very Long Ways from 240,000 Miles to the Moon, which would Require no less

(HOW all People can Prosper in a RIIT WAA, and Stop Polluting the Earth with Capitalist TRASH!)

than 14 Days to get there, if those AstroNAUGHTIES were Traveling at 17,000 MpH, and another 14 Days to Return in Safe Condition at the same Speed. However, no one has Explained just HOW they got themselves going at 80,000 MpH, in Order to supposedly get there in only 3 DAYS! And then, without any Magic Wands, when they Departed from the Moon, they had to somehow get the Lunar Command Module (Columbia) going 80,000 MpH, just to Return within 3 Days. Yes, they had to Orbit the Moon 30 Times at 4,000 MpH, and then Latch onto the Lunar Module (Eagle), which "blasted off" of the Moon at an Imaginary 4,000 MpH with a Propane Tank of Magic Gas or Rocket Fuel, and Rendezvoused with the Command Module, and then pick up Speed without a Rocket Launcher, whereby they were Traveling at about 80,000 MpH, if you can Believe it?! I cannot. (See *Wikipedia* for the Proof!) †§‡§§

14-05 [_] O Selected King, we had better Stick with the Subject of Swangkeenomiks: because those Fake Moon Landings could get us into Eternal Arguments without the AID of "**The GREAT Worldwide Televised Court Hearing!**" Yes, that is a Primary Subject that should be brought to COURT, just to Prove whether or not Joshua was an Honest Person, or a Typical Red Jew LIAR!

14-06 [_] Well, I Agree with you 100% — except for the Fact that Swangkeenomiks Requires HONESTY, which is something that we cannot Find in the *Wickedpedia,* which has no Explanation for HOW Men Returned from the Moon, even if they got there; but, I do not Personally Believe that they ever got there: beCause they did not Prove it. Moreover, we have very Powerful Telescopes, which can take Pictures of Far Away Planets; but, for some Strange Reason, they cannot Zero in on the Remains of the Lunar Rovers, which would Stick Out like Sore Thumbs, you might say, IF they were ON the Moon. However, you cannot go to an Observatory and See them: beCause they are NOT there! †§‡

14-07 [_] O Selected King, if a Pea-brain Peacock like you can Punch Holes in the Official Story about the Lunar Landings, just Imagine what a thousand Top Scientists, Engineers, and Specialists could do with all of the "FACTS" at their Disposal: beCause of Holding "**The GREAT Worldwide TELEVISED Court HEARING!**" Yes, those Phony NASA Officials and the Anti-Christ False COVER-UP Federal Government would be SHREDDED and TRASHED! After all, there is no Way on the Moon, nor even within anyone's Good Imagination, that a 5-gallon Propane Tank of Rocket Fuel could have BOOSTED a 2-ton Lunar Module OFF of the Moon at 4,000 MpH! However, if anyone Imagines that it can be Done, they should be the First to Volunteer such a Trick right here on the Good Old Earth! Yes, the Earth has about 6 Times as much Gravity as the Moon has. Therefore, we will be Generous, and put 10 Times as much Rocket Fuel in their Experimental Spacecraft, and thus Discover whether or not they can get it going at 4,000 MpH' without Running OUT of Fuel! Indeed, the Saturn V Rocket Launcher was 363 feet Tall and 33 feet in diameter, and carried no less than a Million Pounds, and came in 3 Stages, which anyone can read about in *Wikipedia,* which is most Interesting: beCause it Required that Great Rocket Launcher to get UP to the Moon, while it only Required a 5-gallon Propane Tank of Gas to Return from the Moon at a Dead Stop! Therefore, someone is LYING to us. Moreover, if anyone Fails to Check the above Box, that Person is Suspect of being an IDIOT! Yes, the Impossibility of it is Obvious to a Thinking Person: beCause the Lunar Command Module (Columbia) was no Tinker Toy. (See *Lunar Orbit Rendezvous* in *Wikipedia,* and *Apollo Command/Service Module.* Notice in the Specifications that the Design Life was 14 Days. There are also very Interesting Drawings of the Service Module, which show the two 40-inch Spherical Oxygen Tanks, and the Fuel Tank, which is also about 40 inches in diameter, and might hold all of one hundred gallons of Fuel, which could hardly get such a Spaceship going 80,000 MpH! But, if you Think so, let us take it to COURT! †§‡§§)

14-08 [_] There is no Doubt in my Mind that the Moon Landings were FAKED: beCause there is a Mountain of Provable Evidence on the Internet to Prove it. Therefore, Swangkeenomiks Rules the Roost on that one, while the Capitalist Liars should be put Out of Business, beginning with NASA (National Aeronautics and Space Administration), who are as Phony as Liars come. †§‡

14-09 [_] O Selected King, I would say that if anyone does not Check the above Box for Verse 14-08, such a Person should be made to Prove you to be WRong, or else have his or her Head Removed with a Broadax. †§‡

14-10 [_] And, is that something that you would Want Done to YOU, if you did not Agree with me about something? Not hardly. Why not just allow Ignorant People to Believe whatever they Want to? However, if they were Perfectly Honest, they would Investigate into the Details about those so-called "Moon Landings," and thus Discover the MOONHOAX Websites: because there are Plenty of them, and not without Good Reasons, which can be Proven in a Courtroom. After all, millions of Honest People would not Believe such Landings to be Hoaxes, if they were not. Nevertheless, all such People are called "Conspiracy Theorists," whereby they are "Branded" as the "BAD GUYS," even as it is for 10,000+ Architects and Engineers who Agree with me that World Trade Center Towers (WTC) 1, 2 and 7 were brought down by EXPLOSIVES, and God knows what else: beCause, in all of History, not ONE High-rise Concrete and Steel Structure has Fallen by Means of FIRES, which is WHY they are Constructed the Way they are: beCause it WORKS. Yes, the Idea has been Tested hundreds of Times by FIRES, and only in the Cases of the WTC Towers 1, 2 and 7 did anyone Claim that Fires brought them down, which were Obviously FALSE Claims made by a LYING Federal Cover-up Government, which should be Arrested for TREASON, Conspiracies, Murders, Deceptions, False Flag Operations and LIES. After all, they are the Unholy Ones who SWORE to Uphold the Constitution, and to Defend the United States of America from ALL Enemies, both Foreign and Domestic; but, during September 11th, 2001, "the greatest Air Force in the world" was SLEEPING, and George Warmonger Bush was reading a Goat Book to School Children, even 7 Minutes after he was Informed about the Attack: beCause he was Obviously in on the Conspiracy, himself, even if he did not Realize how BAD it would Turn Out. Most likely the Lying Red Jews who set it all up had told Lies to George, in which Case, if he Confesses whatever they told him, we can Forgive him. Otherwise, we can Hang him High on an Electric Pole with Little Dick Cheney, Donald Rumsfeld, Paul Wolfwits, Condoosleezee Rice Patty, and whomever else was in on it, and for the Murders of more than a Million People from here to Iraq, Afghanistan, Pakistan, Iran, Syria, and wherever. †§‡

14-11 [_] O Selected King, this seems to be the Fortieth Time that you have brought up that Insane Subject about the Conspiracy of September 11th, 2001. Therefore, if you bring it up again, I am going to Stop Reading your Books: beCause I am getting Sick of Hearing about it. †§‡

14-12 [_] Okay, if I can Remember it, I Promise to not bring it up again, except maybe as a Footnote in a New Book. Remember that this Book was written AFTER Books 040, and 043. Therefore, if you find it again in those Books, just Try to Ignore it. After all, the Truth about it has become an Obsession with me, and with many other Honest People: beCause we cannot Rest in Peace with so many Criminals Running Loose, who should be Locked Up in Maximum Security

Prisons, if they do not Confess the Whole Truth, whatever it might be. Granted, no certain one of them could possibly Know ALL of the Details about whatever Happened during September 11th, 2001: beCause too many Things Happened for it to be Organized and Carried Out by just ONE Master Mind. Indeed, like going to the Moon Hoax, it Required no less than 400,000 People Working on it, and not one of them had ALL of the Details. In Fact, only a very few People Knew what Actually Happened during September 11th, 2001, and they would be the Men who Set Up the EXPLOSIVES, unless the Explosives were still in their Unmarked Boxes, which could have been set down near to whatever Steel Columns needed to be Removed by Remote Control. Whatever the Case, all of the Pieces of the Puzzle can be Fitted Together, and True Justice can be Served at that Great Meeting of the Most Intelligent Minds. Otherwise, the Criminals will go Unpunished, and other Criminals may Try to pull off similar Tricks, unto our own Shame, which is Symbolized by the Bloody Red Stripes on the American Flag, or Deceptive Rag.

14-13 [_] O Selected King, there must be upwards of a thousand books about the Evil Events of September 11th, 2001, and not one of them even Mentions **"The GREAT Worldwide TELEVISED Court HEARING!"** So, is that beCause they are Afraid of it, or just have not Heard about it?

14-14 [_] Well, most of those books were written Years Ago, and therefore most of them are Ignored, while my Inspired Books are still NEW and Fresh, and even Packed with Reasonable Solutions for all of our Massive Problems. However, having so many Capitalized Words in my Books, most "educated" People are "turned off" to them, even as they should be: because they are not Worthy to Escape from the Great Tribulation, much less Live in the Holy City of the Great King! {See www.Amazon.com for: **"The Secret City of the Great King!" (HOW the True Church will Escape from the Great Tribulation!) By The Worldwide People's Revolution!®** Book 042.}

— Chapter 15 —

Will Honest People Escape from the Great Tribulation?

15-01 [_] O Selected King, your Inspired Books Address a Multitude of Important Subjects, which no other Books on the Earth Address with such Diversity of Thoughts. In Fact, I will dare say that few People have ever had such an Extensive Education as you have had. Therefore, I would like to Hear HOW you came about all such Information, since it cannot be found in Popular books, anywhere?

15-02 [_] Well, many of the Great Ideas within my Inspired Books came Directly from "GOD," if you can Believe it. Yes, I give to him all of the Credit and Glory for whatever Truths that one might Discover within my Inspired Books, including the Truths about Swangkeenomiks, which are Inclusive of those **"GLORIOUS Swanky Hotels Castles and Fortresses,"** which have more than 5,000 Advantages over normal Cities of Confusion, which is an Amazing Revelation from God: beCause all such Beautiful Planned City States have ZERO Disadvantages! Indeed, Cars have no less than 40 Great Disadvantages; but, at the same Time, they have at least 2 Great Advantages. For Example, they are quite Reliable for getting you to Work on Time — that is, if there is not a Great Traffic Jam along the Way, which there is about 40% of the Time. Therefore, if you just Ignore the 40 Great Disadvantages — such as Riding in a Known Deathtrap — you can Tolerate the Inconvenience of getting to Work Late, and getting Home Late. However, during the Judgment Day, God will say: "Did you not Know that Automobiles were an Abomination to me? Did you not Study: **'The Nature of CAPITALISM!' (A List of the EVILS of CAPITALISM!) By The Worldwide People's Revolution!®**, Book 038?" And then you will Hang your Head with Shame: because, God will say: "DEPART from me, you Workers of Iniquities: beCause I never Knew you. Indeed, you did not Do anything that I Asked of you with a True Heart." And thus you will be Cast OUT! †§‡

15-03 [_] O Selected King, that is Absolutely FRIGHTENING! Indeed, if anyone takes it Seriously, he or she will be Struck Down with GRIEF for his or her SINS: beCause of Learning that NO Unclean Thing shall Enter into the Holy Kingdom of All that is GOOD, which just Naturally Includes those Stinking Noisy Polluting CARS, Vans, Pickups, Trucks, Buses, Lawnmowers, Chainsaws, Weed-eaters, Garden Tillers, Snow Blowers, Snowmobiles, Motorcycles, Motor Scooters, Motorboats, 4-Wheelers, and whatever STINKS and makes Horrible NOISES. †‡

15-04 [_] Well, each Person must Try to Live with his or her own Conscience; but, Capitalism makes it Extremely Difficult to Do so, which might Explain WHY tens of thousands of those Capitalists Commit Suicide, each Year! Yes, their Consciences are Racked with GUILT for all of their SINS, which are Transgressions of the Laws of God. Therefore, there is only one Hope for them, and that is that they will Learn the Whole Truth, Confess it, and REPENT. Otherwise, they will have to Suffer through the Great Tribulation, which will be no Fun at all: beCause of the Seven Last Great Plagues, which you can read about in Chapter 11.

15-05 [_] O Selected King, it is my Sincere Belief that we are already in the Great Tribulation, and you do not Realize it: beCause Things are not so BAD as they could be — that is, for YOU; but, for ME, they are as Bad as Things could get! †§‡

15-06 [_] You have got to be Kidding! Things could get a hundred Times WORSE, and for most everyone on the Earth! For Example, suppose the Temperature RISES by 30 Degrees, Worldwide — what in the World would you Do to COOL OFF in August, if you Live in the Northern Hemisphere? Moreover, suppose the Ocean RISES by 20 Meters — what in the World will the People in Coastal Cities DO to Survive it? Trust me, there are not Enough Caves in the Mountains to Move into, much less a 20-year Supply of Foods in those Caves. And that could be just the Beginning of Sorrows for Ignorant Citiots, who have no Idea HOW to Grow their own Foods, even if they were Given the Land to Grow those Foods on! Therefore, all such People have gotten themselves into "Pickle Barrels," you might say, with no Way to Climb Out: beCause Satan has them TRAPPED. Yes, even I am also Trapped: beCause I was Forced to Sell the Farm and Move into a City of Confusion, just to Survive: beCause it was Costing a hundred Dollars just to fill up the Gas Tank to get to Town to Buy such Things as Water Pumps, Pipes, Fittings, Cement, and whatever. For Example, some Varmint managed to crawl into the 3-inch Water Pipe, which was a quarter of a Mile Long, and it Died and Swelled Up and Plugged Up the Water Pipe. So, I contacted a Friendly Naaber, who figured that he could "blow the pipe out" if he connected the Fire Hose to

(HOW all People can Prosper in a RIIT WAA, and Stop Polluting the Earth with Capitalist TRASH!)

it from the Fire Truck, which he Kindly did for Free; and the Water Pressure BROKE the Pipe in 3 Places, which Required the next Month to Discover those Places and Dig Up the Pipe for 30 feet on each Side of each Break, and then Fix them, at which Time the Dead Creature had Rotted and passed on through, which it would have done for Free, if we had Known that it was in there, and just left the Pipe and the Water alone, and not even Turned on the Pump. However, the All-Mineral Orgimmick Garden needed Watering; and therefore, it was only Logical to Turn On the Pump, and without Realizing that it would Cost a thousand Dollars to Fix it, and also Require a Month of Hard Work! And that was just a Minor Thing. Yes, you should Hear about a Major Thing that Happened, which I Reported in: **"The KO$T of a DIPSTIK!"** Yes, it ran into the MILLIONS of Dollars! †§‡ {See: **"An Amazing Collection of Wit and Wisdom!" (The Marvelous Tale of the Colorful Peacock from Angel Ridge, and the Strong Rope of Everlasting Hope!) By The Worldwide People's Revolution!®** Book 048.}

15-07 [_] O Selected King, I have Heard of that Famous Story before; but, I cannot Remember just WHERE it came from. Can you Help me to Find it?

15-08 [_] Well, it will be Easy to Find, if we Hold **"The GREAT Worldwide TELEVISED Court HEARING"**: beCause we can simply ASK if anyone has it; and therefore, if they do have it, we can Discover it, which is also True for a LOT of Things that Need to be Discovered — such as whether or not the Earth is Actually HOLLOW!? Yes, that Sounds Interesting to me. However, most Americans just Assume that if it were Hollow, they would be able to read about it in the Public School of Ignorant FOOLS. But, for **"The KO$T of a DIPSTIK,"** one only needs to See the Note in Verse 15-06. {See www.Amazon.com for: **"The Public School of IGNERUNT FQLZ!" (HOW we have been GRAATLEE DISEEVD by Capitalism!)**, Book 024, plus: **"Are you a Jobless Graduate of the SKQL uv FQLZ?" (HOW to get a GOUD EJUKAASHUN without Robbing the Bank!) By The Worldwide People's Revolution!®** Book 020.}

15-09 [_] O Selected King, if only Honest People can Escape from the Great Tribulation, just HOW in the World will we go about becoming Honest People, when we are Habitual LIARS? For Example, when someone asks me How I am, I say: "I'm good, thank you; and how are you?" And that Person usually says something like it, when it is NOT the Truth, at all. In Fact, if I Confessed all that is WRong with me, it would fill up a Newspaper, or at least a Page or 2. Therefore, I will not Bother you with my Ailments at this Time: beCause I am Sure that you get my Point. Yes, it would be Em-bare-assing to be Overly Honest, since a lot of my Problems are concerning my Private Parts: because I Suffer with Chronic Constipation of the Mind, you might say, and have not Studied: **"Did God or Satan Ordain Medical Doctors??" (Ask Huck Finn and/or Nigger Jim: because neither Tom Sawyer nor Judge Thatcher would Know!) By The Worldwide People's Revolution!®** Book 022. Moreover, speaking of Sex, I have something to say about the Judge Brett Kavanaugh Case in the District of Chief Criminals, in Washington. It is a well-known Fact that some Drunk People cannot Remember what they said nor did when they were Drunk, and especially when they were not Traumatized by a Sex Offender, as was the Case for Professor Christine Blasey Ford, who had no Trouble Remembering his Aggressions on her, when she was only 15 Years Old, while it was all just a Joke to Altar Boy Brett and his Friend Mark Judge, who has Obviously Lied about Traumatizing her, even without Realizing that he has Lied: beCause of not Remembering his Evil Deed in the Upper Room at the Unholy Church of Graceful Sinners on Drunkard's Avenue and Sexually Curious Lane, while the not-so-Sweet Jungle Music was Playing

Loudly to help Cover Up the Lip-smacking Ball-clapping Erotic Fun, Upstairs on the Convenient Bed of Lusts, next to the Condom Dispenser on the Wall, which is still Covered with Artistic Drawings of Fully Erect Stallions, who are full of Milk Pales of Hot Fragrant Sperm and Delicious Semen, which could have and should have been Deposited in Senator Grassley's Coffee Cup for Seasoning, who knows for Sure that a Full Investigation should be made by the Federal Burden of Investigations (FBI) and the Central Unintelligent Agencies (CIA), just to Clear Out the Stink in the Courtroom. However, in spite of Lying about it — Consciously or Unconsciously — Brett Kavanaugh can still Redeem himself, and become a Supreme Court Injustice, just by making a Full Confession of his Drunken Parties, Sexual Aggressions, and whatever Sins he has ever Committed in his own Mind, as Jesus would say, whereby we will all Know for a Fact that he is perhaps the one and only HONEST Supreme Court Justice, which will make him more Trustworthy than the other Injustices, who did not even Investigate the Evil Events of September 11th, 2001, nor DEMAND a Full and Unbiased Investigation by the French, German, British, Russian, and Chinese Investigators, who would have no doubt Discovered the Thermite Residues of EXPLOSIVES at the World Trade Center Buildings in Dusty New Yuck City, along with the Melted Cars by Microwave Energy, even as Dr. Judy Wood Proved in her Video Recordings in YouTube Websites, which Evidences are Confirmed by thousands of Architects and Engineers at: www.AE911TRUTH.org and "**Experts Speak Out**" Videos, which the Low Court of Supreme Injustices simply IGNORE! †§‡§§

15-10 [ ] Well, to be Perfectly Honest at all Times and in all Places could Prove to be Fatal, if you were around the WRong People. Therefore, it does Require Discretion and Discernment. {See www.Amazon.com for: **"Thu Nq MAGNUFIID Verzhun uv Thu PROVERBZ uv KING SOLUMUN in Plaan Ingglish!" (The Understandable Version of the Famous Proverbs of King Solomon in Plain English!) By The Worldwide People's Revolution!®** Book 028.} However, in the Case of Judge Brett Kavanaugh, he is no doubt Sincerely Innocent in his own Mind: beCause, according to the Best of his Drunken Memory, he did nothing that he is Accused of, which could be the Case in Reality. I would not Know for a Fact; but, I do Know for a Fact that none of that Nonsense would have ever Happened Inside of a First Class Swanky Fortress: beCause of not Drinking Alcoholic Beverages, like Beers. Moreover, at the Hearing, Brett Defended his Reputation as a Good Man, without any Idea concerning just Exactly what a "GOOD" Man might be, who would Certainly not be Attending Bars and Restaurants with Drunkards and Gluttons, even if Jesus did it on certain Occasions, who was also called a Friend of Gluttons and Drunkards. However, it is my Guess that he got them Converted from their Evil Ways, rather than becoming one with them in Spirit and in Reality. Moreover, I am Sure that Judge Kavanaugh would not put himself into a Category with Jesus nor any of the Saints, even as I would not. However, his Testimony is Clearly a Condemnation of Drinking Parties, which he still seems to be Trying to Justify, as if that were an American Virtue, when it is Actually one of our Greatest Weaknesses. Indeed, try to Imagine a Drunk Supreme Court making Decisions about anything. Perhaps that is what is WRong with them? Perhaps that is WHY they did not Call for a Thorough Investigation of ALL of the Evil Events of September 11th, 2001? Perhaps that is WHY they are not Defending those **"GLORIOUS Swanky Hotels Castles and Fortresses!" (Beautiful Planned City States for WISE Intelligent Well-Educated People with Common Sense and Good Understanding!) By The Worldwide People's Revolution!®, Book 019**? Perhaps that is WHY their Priorities are Out of Order? Perhaps that is what is WRong with the entire Washington Swamp? Perhaps they are all Drunk on Drugs, except for Senator Sober Honesty and Congressman Truth Seeker. I would not Know for Sure; but, I do Know that it all Calls for a Thorough Investigation and Confession.‡

15-11 [_] O Selected King, I much Prefer **"The New MAGNIFIED Version of The Book of MORMON!" (The Story of the White and Dark Indians in the Americas!)**, Book 040, plus: **"Terrorists Beware that your Days are Numbered!" (HOW to Bring those Terrorist Attacks to a Screeching HALT!) By The Worldwide People's Revolution!®**, Book 043, which contains *the Book of LEHI,* which is one of my Favorite Books, which is Small and Beautiful.

15-12 [_] Well, no one Knows what might be Found in my Inspired Books, until they Read them with a Capital R — as in Carefully, Prayerfully, Thoughtfully, and with a Good Sense of Humor. Yes, they should Study: **"The PRAYERS of PUMPKINHEADS!" (Even God Needs a Little Humor to Cheer himself Up!)**, Book 007, as well as: **"AIIRMWVC and Reasonable Solutions!" (Aliens, Illegal Immigrants, Refugees, Migrant Workers and other Victims of Capitalism!)**, Book 032, plus: **"A Sure Cure for GUN VIOLENCE!" (HOW TO STOP GANG WARS and CRIMINAL SHOOTINGS!)**, Book 031, plus: **"ECCLESIASTES UNCOVERED!" (The New MAGNIFIED Version of Ecclesiastes and the Song of Solomon in Plain English!) By The Worldwide People's Revolution!®** Book 034.

— Chapter 16 —

The Conclusion

16-01 [_] Trust me, this is NOT the "Last Word" about Swangkeenomiks, which is Bound to become a very HOT Topic among the Masses of People during the near Future: beCause this is a Brand New Idea, which the People of the World have never Considered before, or else they might now be Living within those **"GLORIOUS Swanky Hotels Castles and Fortresses!" (Beautiful Planned City States for WISE Intelligent Well-Educated People with Common Sense and Good Understanding!) By The Worldwide People's Revolution!®** Book 019. {NOTE: Be Sure to Read about those **"Beautiful Swanky PALACES!" (A New Concept in Living Habits — Swanky Palaces for Poor People!)**, Book 066, which is a Companion Book of: **"The Environmentalists' Paradise!" (HOW almost Everyone could be Living in a Beautiful Manmade Paradise!)**, Book 035.}

16-02 [_] So, O Selected King, if your Inspired Books Require any Updating during the Future, WHO will Update them when you are Dead and Gone?

16-03 [_] Well, a few of the so-called "Facts" might Change, and Names might even be Forgotten a hundred Years or so from now; but, generally-speaking, the Truths will Remain Permanent; and therefore, no one will have to Update my Inspired Books, once they are Perfected. Indeed, if there are any Errors, we can get them Corrected at **"The GREAT Worldwide TELEVISED Court HEARING!"** {See www.Amazon.com for: **"The New MAGNIFIED Version of the Book of ACTS!" (The Understandable Version of the ACTS of the Apostles!)**, Book 063, which gives a much more Thorough Explanation of Swangkeenomiks than all other Books, combined, and in a Beautiful Way. Indeed, it is a Diamond-rated Book, while this one is only a Heart-rated Book, which Means that it is Extremely Good, while this one is only Exceptionally Good, and only beCause of the Quotations from Magnified Versions of Scriptures — such as the Story of the Prodigal Son, which also has a Diamond-rating, which is a bit Out of Place in this Book; but, it is the Reason for that Heart-rating. Otherwise, this Book would only have a Star or Fair Rating with a Square: beCause it does not go into the Fine Details about Swangkeenomiks, which could possibly be Defined in just one Beautiful Sentence, which should be Posted on the Front Doors of all Public Buildings, including all Schools, Churches, Courthouses, Businesses, and Government Buildings, Worldwide —

> **Swangkeenomiks is an Economic System that does not Depend on the Exploitation of Limited Natural Resources, nor of Poor Ignorant People, who are Deliberately made into Education Slaves, Work Slaves, Tax Slaves, Insurance Slaves, Interest Slaves, Transportation Slaves, Food Bills Slaves, Gas Bills Slaves, Water Bills Slaves, ElecTrickery Bills Slaves, Entertainment Bills Slaves, Drug Slaves, and Endless Bills Slaves for the Sake of Enriching a few Rich Hogs, while the Masses of People go on Suffering in their Depressed States of Extreme Poverty, who do not even have Fresh Clean Air to Breathe, Pure Living Water to Drink, Wholesome Natural Foods to Eat, nor Secure Fireproof, Mouse-proof, Rat-proof, Flood-proof, Tornado-proof, Rot-proof, Paint-proof, Termite-proof, Hurricane-proof, Mudslide-proof, Earthquake-proof, Insurance-proof, nor Tax-proof and Self-air-conditioned Stone Dome Home Complexes to Live in, which everyone in the Whole World could have and should have — Thanks to that Great Generous Creator God, who Provided all Natural Material Resources for all of us to Richly Enjoy and Share with one another, without making SLAVES of ourselves, nor of anyone else: because we now have Mechanical Slaves for doing the Difficult Work, who, as Voluntary Working Soldiers, could do so little as 4 Hours of Common Skilled Labor per Day, or the Equivalent thereof, in Exchange for Living within "Beautiful Swanky PALACES" with "Royal Swanky Buffets," and whatever Beautiful Things that we are Willing to Work for, without any Loans of Money, without any Interest / Usury, and without any Taxes, in spite of Earning FAIR Swanky Wages: beCause of Electing a Righteous King to Govern "The New RIGHTEOUS One-World Government!" (HOW to Establish a Righteous One-World Government without Going to WAR!), Book 056, which can be Accomplished by the Masses of People DEMANDING: "The GREAT Worldwide TELEVISED Court HEARING," whereby the Whole Truth can be Revealed about each Important Subject, including a Proper Lifestyle for Humanity, which is Basically a "Garden of Eden" Lifestyle, as Opposed to a "City of Confusion" Lifestyle, whereby X-amount of Criminals are Produced, as Opposed to Innocent Christ-like Lambs of God, who are Free with a Capital F, being Healthy, Wealthy, and WISE!**

16-04 [_] O Elected King, I Sense that you are getting into a Hurry to Finish this Good Book, which Needs at least one more Good Sermon to Light our Fires. Therefore, can you not be Patient, and get it Done for us?

16-05 [_] Well, I have many more Books to Write, and this one is Long Enough for one Day of Reading, which could be "red" within 2 Days within Churches, if anyone is Interested in it. After all, I am probably the only Person in the Whole World who Reveals WHERE to go to, in Order to Escape from the Great Tribulation! (See Verse 14-14.)

(HOW all People can Prosper in a RIIT WAA, and Stop Polluting the Earth with Capitalist TRASH!)

16-06 [_] O Selected King, if anyone Vainly Imagines that Swangkeenomiks is BAD, they just need to hang around until Babylon FALLS, and the Great False Economy CRASHES, and they are left under 20 Meters of Rising Tides in Missouri, Kansas, Nebraska, Iowa, and South Dakota! Yes, those Glorious Swanky Fortresses will Look rather Appealing during those Days!

16-07 [_] O Selected King, the Energy that is now Wasted in Vehicles running around on Endless Highways should be used Wisely to Build those **"Beautiful Swanky PALACES"** for everyone in the World, and then no Swanky Fortresses will be Needed: beCause everyone will be Moderately RICH. †§‡

16-08 [_] Well, my Friend, that is a Pleasant Thought; but, you have not Thought it all through: beCause you would have Raccoons Eating your Sweet Corn in your Gardens: beCause of not having those TALL STRONG STONE WALLS around your Swanky Palaces. Moreover, you would not have those Wind Generators, millions of large Cisterns, nor SECURE Cities, if Wars should break out among all such Ignorant Fools. Indeed, the Swanky Fortresses have thousands of Advantages that Swanky Palaces might not have, all alone. But, those Palaces are very Good on the Insides of the Fortresses, where they can be Protected, and especially in the Castles. Therefore, you should Study the entire Master Plan, before coming to any Irrational Conclusions. ‡

16-09 [_] O Elected King, if everyone in the World should simply Submit to **"The Swanky Sword of Divine Truths,"** it would not be long before everyone would be Moderately RICH, with or without any FAIR Swanky Wages. †§‡

16-10 [_] Well, my Friend, only the Whole Truth can Liberate us from our Prison of Lies, and that Whole Truth must be Learned at: **"The GREAT Worldwide TELEVISED Court HEARING!" (That Great Meeting of the Most Intelligent and Well-Educated Minds!) By The Worldwide People's Revolution!®** Book 041. Therefore, that is the next Step on the Highway of LIFE, which has a Priority over everything else that is Happening in this World of Wonders and Woes. {See: **"HOW to Get our PRIORITIES in ORDER!" (The Glories of Democracy; and, Does DEMON-ocracy have its Priorities in Order?) By The Worldwide People's Revolution!®** Book 060.} Therefore, make this a Good Day by Spreading this Message around in your Naaberhoud. Challenge your Friends, Relatives and Naaberz to Collect the ONE-MILLION-DOLLAR REWARD that is Offered by Amazon to anyone who can Prove my **"Guaranteed Solutions!"** to be WRong or Unworkable. (See the Description at www.Amazon.com.)

A Long List of other Fascinating Literature by the same Inspired Author

[_] 40-01 — "LIGHTNING Versus the Lightning Bug!" (HOW almost Everyone can become Moderately RICH, without Telling Any Lies nor Selling Any Trash!) Book 001.

[_] 40-02 — "What is WRong with those Professing Christians?" (A Self-Examination of the Heart of the Body of Good Government!) Book 002.

[_] 40-03 — "For the Love of Money!" (The Strange Things that People Say and Do to Get more Money!) Book 003.

[_] 40-04 — "HOW to Prepare for CLIMATE CHANGES!" (The Wisest Plan for Mankind to Follow!) Book 004.

[_] 40-05 — "Why do I have to be Surrounded by CRAZY PEOPLE!" (Do almost all People Feel like they are Surrounded by CRAZY People??) Book 005.

[_] 40-06 — "The Washington Journal is a FARCE! (C-SPAN Managers are not very WISE!) Book 006. (This Book has lots of Good Humor.)

[_] 40-07 — "The PRAYERS of PUMPKINHEADS!" (Even God Needs a Little Humor to Cheer himself Up!) Book 007. (Some of it is for Adults only.)

[_] 40-08 — "A Sound Argument for Masters and Servants!" (WHY Everyone Needs a Good Master, and every Master Needs Good Obedient Servants!) Book 008.

[_] 40-09 — "WHY are some Preachers so POOR?" (HOW almost all Preachers could Get Moderately RICH, without Preaching any Outlandish LIES!) Book 009.

[_] 40-10 — "GOOD NEWS for REBEL WOMEN!" (HOW almost all Wives can become Moderately RICH without Leaving their Homes! Guaranteed!) Book 010.

[_] 40-11 — "The Low Court of Supreme Injustices is Brought to Trial!" (The Worldwide People's Revolution!® Butts Heads with the United States Supreme Court, with or without their Black Robes of Hypocrisies and Lies!) Book 011. (This Inspired Book contains the Famous *Declaration of Interdependence,* which is a Must Read. It also contains the Correct Wording for the Placard on the Statue of Liberty.)

[_] 40-12 — "The Right Design for Living!" (A List of Great Advantages for Building Beautiful Planned City States!) Book 012. (This Book contains many Important Drawings, as well as HOW to Save hundreds of Trillions of Dollars by Building Swanky Fortresses, and Living in Peace within them. It is a Companion Book of Book 011, which contains many more Great Advantages for Fortresses.)

(HOW all People can Prosper in a RIIT WAA, and Stop Polluting the Earth with Capitalist TRASH!)

[_] 40-13 — **"The Gospel According to The Worldwide People's Revolution!® " (The Good News from the Most Modern Perspective!)** Book 013. (This Book contains the Famous Sermon of Jonah to the Ninevites, whereby 120,000 People Repented in Sackcloth and Ashes! Do not Miss Out on it.)

[_] 40-14 — **"Poverty Hunger Riots Strikes Brutalities Election Deceptions and Civil Wars!" (The High Price that we Earthlings have Paid for Leaving the Good Land!)** Book 014.

[_] 40-15 — **"Seven Great Armies of Working Soldiers!" (HOW to Provide a Way for Everyone to WORK: so as to Eliminate Poverty, Crimes, Drug Abuses, Prisons and Unnecessary Taxes!)** Book 015. (This Book contains a True Life Story when I was in the Army.)

[_] 40-16 — **"The CONSTITUTION for the New RIGHTEOUS One-World GovernMint!" (HOW all Peoples can get True Justice, and Celebrate the Great Year of JUBILEE!)** Book 016.

[_] 40-17 — **"The Great World TEMPLE of PEACE!" (The Glory of Jerusalem Arises Again!) By The Worldwide People's Revolution!®** Book 017.

[_] 40-18 — **"The Swanky Associations of Working Soldiers!" (A Fascinating Collection of Various Kinds of Voluntary Working Soldiers!)** Book 018. (There will be thousands of Associations for all Kinds of Occupations, which will Specialize in Fine Arts — such as Hand-carved Leather-bound Books. See **"LIGHTNING STRIKES Versus Lightning Bugs!"** Book 074, for a Good Example.)

[_] 40-19 — **"GLORIOUS Swanky Hotels Castles and Fortresses!" (Beautiful Planned City States for WISE Intelligent Well-Educated People with Common Sense and Good Understanding!)** Book 019. (This Book contains many Rough Drawings, which could be Greatly Improved upon by someone who Knows the Art, and has the Correct Computer Programs for doing it.)

[_] 40-20 — **"Are you a Jobless Graduate of the SKQL uv FQLZ?" (HOW to Get a GOUD EJUKAASHUN without Robbing the Bank!)** Book 020. (This Inspired Book contains the New MAGNIFIED Version {NMV} of *First Corinthians 13*, plus: HOW to Produce Pure Living Water!)

[_] 40-21 — **"The LUSCIOUS All-Mineral Organic Method of Gardening!" (HOW to Grow DELICIOUS Satisfying Foods for Potential Kingz and Kweenz in Beautiful Swanky PALACES!)** Book 021. (This Book Explains HOW to make a Flood-proof Garden, while Trapping the Rainwater.)

[_] 40-22 — **"Did God or Satan Ordain Medical Doctors?" (Ask Huck Finn and/or Nigger Jim: because neither Tom Sawyer nor Judge Thatcher would Know!)** Book 022. (This Inspired Book Reveals HOW to Prevent Common Colds, and has a Special Chapter that Explains what a True "Nigger" IS. Surprise yourself!)

[_] 40-23 — **"The BIG White OUTHOUSE on the Not-so-Biblical Capitol DUNGHILL!" (The Chief Sins of the Divided States of United Lies!) By The Worldwide People's Revolution!®** Book 023. (This Book contains Special Words that most People have never Heard! Surprise yourself again!)

[_] 40-24 — **"The Public School of IGNERUNT FQLZ!" (HOW we have been GRAATLEE DISEEVD by Capitalism!)** Book 024. (This Book Teaches Children HOW to "Reed and Riit in Funetik Ingglish in just wun Daa!" You should Challenge your Frendz and Naaberz with it.)

[_] 40-25 — **"In thu Beeginingz uv Thingz!" (Thu Kreeaashun Stooree frum thu Beegining!)** Book 025. {The Cover Photo shows a Picture of a Golden Supootaa (Sapote), which not one Person in a Million has ever Tasted: because it does not Ship very well, in spite of it being one of the most Sweetest Pleasant Fruits known to Mankind, which must Ripen on the Tree to be Extremely Good, after it is Grown Properly by **"The LUSCIOUS All-Mineral Organic Method of Gardening!"** Book 021, which Means that the Topsoil must have all of the Proper Minerals in it. Remember the Grapes of Eschol, which the Children of Israel brought back from the Promised Land in the *Book of Joshua,* which Required 2 Strong Men to Carry just one Cluster! See the Fascinating Photos in: **"Orgimmick Gardening at its Best!" (HOW to Grow Delicious Satisfying Foods without a 10-Million-Dollar Investment!) By The Worldwide People's Revolution!®** Book 079.}

[_] 40-26 — **"God Speaks and the Whole World Listens!" (Fire on the Mountain from the Burning Bush by the Spirit of Truths!)** Book 026. (This Powerful Book contains the Best Noah Story of all of the Books, including that of Gilgamesh the Great of Ancient Babylon!)

[_] 40-27 — **"Does a Good Soldier have to be a MURDERER?" (Seven Great Swanky Armies of Voluntary Working Soldiers!) By The Worldwide People's Revolution!®** Book 027. (Chapter 03 contains a True Life Story about a Dog Pile, which happened to me when I was just 10 Years Old.)

[_] 40-28 — **"Thu Nq MAGNUFIID Verzhun uv Thu PROVERBZ uv KING SOLUMUN in Plaan Ingglish!" (The Understandable Version of the Famous Proverbs of King Solomon in Plain English!)** Book 028. (This Marvelous Book MAGNIFIES each Proverb unto the Glory of the Great God of Inspiration, which is taken from the Original 4,000-page Book, which was written in less than 2 Months by the GIFT of Inspiration, which also contains the Famous Proverbs of Queen Izubelu!)

[_] 40-29 — **"UNLIMITED ENERJEE 99 Percent Pollutions Free!" (HOW to Obtain FREE ElecTrickery, Worldwide!) By The Worldwide People's Revolution!®** Book 029. (This Book contains the Jackson Brower Suicide, among many other Fascinating Subjects.)

[_] 40-30 — **"FREEDUM uv SPEECH!" (U Speshoul Maguzeen uv Onist Upinyunz!)** Book 030-0001, which contains the Great Advantages for Using Swanky Mulching Rocks in an All-Mineral Organic Garden, plus Baptism by Fire and Speaking in Foreign Languages! It is a Must Read. The Cover Photo shows a Portion of the Author's Marbleous Indian Countertop or Food Bar, which is just one Example of what you can also have in your own **"Beautiful Swanky PALACES!"** if you have the Honesty, Faith, Hope, Trust, Love, Patience, Persistence,

Cooperation and OBEDIENCE that are Required for True Prosperity! Therefore, Ejukaat yourself, and you will be Glad that you did!

[_] 40-31 — "A Sure Cure for GUN VIOLENCE!" (HOW TO STOP GANG WARS and CRIMINAL SHOOTINGS!) By The Worldwide People's Revolution!® Book 031. {The Cover Photo shows a Picture of a Short Shotgun, which is Fully Loaded with Double 00 Shells, and is Ready for any Tax Master who might Attempt to Steal the Retirement Home, who never moved a Finger to Help Build the Rock Houses, whereby we moved more than 66,666,666 Pounds by Hand, whose Property was Cunningly Stolen by that False Anti-Christ WICKED Cover-up Government, which allowed Bankers to Rob us of 30 Years of Hard Labor and more than 300,000 dollars-worth of Investments in our Uncommon American Farm, which is Explained in: "LIGHTNING STRIKES Versus Lightning Bugs!" (HOW you can Become Moderately RICH, without Telling any Lies nor Selling any Trash!) By The Worldwide People's Revolution!® Book 074, which contains many Photographs with Profound Explanations! Do not be left out in the Darkness of Ignorance. Get Informed, now: beCause, "The Great False Economy is now DEBUNKED!" Book 053.}

[_] 40-32 — "AIIRMWVC and Reasonable Solutions!" (Aliens, Illegal Immigrants, Refugees, Migrant Workers and other Victims of Capitalism!) By The Worldwide People's Revolution!® Book 032. (This Inspired Book contains *the New MAGNIFIED Version of Job 33*.)

[_] 40-33 — "Mark Twain Races for the PRESIDENCY!" (The 2020 Presidential Candidates Desperately Need Some STRONG Undefeatable COMPETITION!) By The Worldwide People's Revolution!® Book 033. {This Book contains a Part of my Autobiography, and my Personal Answers to the Questions in "The Complete SURVEYS of our VALUES!" (SURVEYS of Religious Spiritual Political Governmental Sexual Social Moral Economic Business Labor Habitual and Miscellaneous VALUES!) Book 059. It also contains many Black and White Photographs.}

[_] 40-34 — "ECCLESIASTES UNCOVERED!" (The New MAGNIFIED Version of Ecclesiastes and the Song of Solomon in Plain English!) Book 034. (This is the Book that contains the Famous Sayings for *"There is a Time to be Born, and a Time to Die ..."* which has been Greatly Magnified!)

[_] 40-35 — "The Environmentalists' Paradise!" (HOW almost Everyone could be Living in a Beautiful Manmade Paradise!) By The Worldwide People's Revolution!® Book 035. (This Book contains the NMV of *Psalm 48,* which will Amaze you, O Lady Doubtfulness!)

[_] 40-36 — "The Seven Basic Spiritual Building Blocks of LIFE!" (Faith Hope Trust Love Patience Persistence and Obedience!) Book 036. (This Book contains the Mockingbird's Version of *Hebrews 11,* plus the NMV of *First Corinthians 13,* among many other "Goodies.")

[_] 40-37 — "DIETS!" (A Reasonable Solution for the "Eternal Controversy"!) By The Worldwide People's Revolution!® Book 037.

[_] 40-38 — "The Nature of CAPITALISM!" (A List of the EVILS of CAPITALISM!) Book 038.

[_] 40-39 — **"SWANGKEENOMIKS Rules the Roost!"** (HOW all People can Prosper in a RIIT WAA, and STOP Polluting the Earth with Capitalist TRASH!) By The Worldwide People's Revolution!® Book 039. (The Cover Photo shows a Portion of our Retirement Home, before the 5,000+ square-feet Concrete Roof was Installed, after moving more than 66 Million Pounds by Hand!)

[_] 40-40 — **"The New MAGNIFIED Version of The Book of MORMON!" (The Story of the White and Dark Indians in the Americas!)** Book 040, which comes in 2 Volumes of about 500 Pages, each. The Cover Photo on the First Volume shows the Queen of England's Golden Coach, and the Cover Photo on the Second Volume shows one of many Polished Spanish Marble Walls in our Selected King's Retirement Home, which is worth a thousand dollars per square yard, which is another Example of what you can also have, if you simply OBEY your Righteous KING! All such Marble is very Inspiring. No one could Study it for very long without Believing in a Great Creator God. The Picture does not do it Justice. You would have to See it in Person, and Wash it with Pure Water to bring Out the Beauty.

[_] 40-41 — **"The GREAT Worldwide TELEVISED Court HEARING!" (That Great Meeting of the Most Intelligent and Wel-Ejukaatid Miindz!)** By The Worldwide People's Revolution!® Book 041. {This is the Book that the World has long been Waiting for: beCause it will Overthrow the Evil Empires, and make it Possible to Establish **"The New RIGHTEOUS One-World Government!" (HOW to Establish a Righteous One-World Government without Going to WAR!)** By The Worldwide People's Revolution!® Book 056. This is the Greatest Idea since the Invention of the Light Bulb, Guaranteed!}

[_] 40-42 — **"The Secret City of the Great King!" (HOW the True Church will Escape from the Great Tribulation!)** By The Worldwide People's Revolution!® Book 042. (Be Sure to Inform your Friends, Relatives and Naaberz about this Wonderful Book: beCause they might also Want to Escape!)

[_] 40-43 — **"Terrorists Beware that your Days are Numbered!"** (HOW to Bring those Terrorist Attacks to a Screeching HALT!) By The Worldwide People's Revolution!® Book 043. (This Book also contains the Fascinating Book of LEHI, which has now been Restored!) †‡

[_] 40-44 — **"The New MAGNIFIED Version of ISAIAH in Plain English!" (The Understandable Version of the Book of Isaiah!)** Book 044. (The Cover Photo shows a Swanky Potato and Avocado Salad with Sweet Peas and Corn, among other "Secret" Ingredients, which are Revealed within the Book. Remember that you can read many Words for Free in the Book Previews on Amazon.com.usa.)

[_] 40-45 — **"HOW to Become a HOLY Man!"** (40 Good Reasons WHY People Should FAST and PRAY!) Book 045, which is a Companion Book of:

[_] 40-46 — **"The Proper RULES for FASTING!" (The Complete Instruction Manual for True Repentance!)** By The Worldwide People's Revolution!® Book 046, which is a Companion Book of the above mentioned Book, which contains a True Life Story about an Old Black Mare called Lucy, who Fasted for 30 Days without Food nor Water, who was Physiologically "Born Again," as Jesus might say. See the Full Details in: **"The New

MAGNIFIED Version of The GOOD NEWS According to Saint JOHN!" (The Gospel According to Saint John Zebedee Boanerges in Plain English!) Book 062, which contains many Inspiring Photographs with Explanations!

[_] 40-47 — **"Are Americans the Most STUPID People who ever Lived?"** (HOW Working People can PROSPER and Live in PEACE Under the Rulership of a RIGHTEOUS KING!) By The Worldwide People's Revolution!® Book 047. (The Cover Photo shows a large Portion of the Author's Living Room Floor, which is worth 100,000$, which is just another Good Example of what you can also have, just for Loving and Obeying your Elected King!)

[_] 40-48 — **"An Amazing Collection of Wit and Wisdom!"** (The Marvelous Tale of the Colorful Peacock from Angel Ridge, and the Strong Rope of Everlasting Hope!) By The Worldwide People's Revolution!® Book 048. (The Cover Photo shows a Book Display, which will be Greatly Enhanced during the Future, when all 350+ Inspired Books are on Display in a Swanky Truth-brary, as Opposed to the Public LIE-brary.)

[_] 40-49 — **"Justifications for Capitalizations!"** (WHY The Worldwide People's Revolution!® Defies the School of Fools by Capitalizing LOVE and HATE!) Book 049.

[_] 40-50 — **"The END of CONFUSION!"** (The Great CELEBRATION of the Magnificent Wedding of the Most Humble Honest Nations, and the Grand Year of JUBILEE!) By The Worldwide People's Revolution!® Book 050. (Just Try to Visualize those **"Seven Great Swanky Armies of Voluntary Working Soldiers"** Marching through the Valley of Megiddo, being Dressed in their Colorful Robes, while the Band Plays *The Battle Hymn of the Republic,* and the Choirs Sing the Praises of the Great KING of Kings! What a Sight and Sound that will be, which will be Climaxed in **"The Great World TEMPLE of PEACE,"** when the Nations will get Married, along with our Elected King! Come one, come all to **"The Great Worldwide TELEVISED Court HEARING,"** by Means of your Wide Flat-screen TVs, whereby you might Learn WHY, WHEN and HOW!) †‡

[_] 40-51 — **"The Loathsome Burdens of the Independent Jackasses!"** (A New Civilized Approach for Quietly Solving our Massive Problems!) By The Worldwide People's Revolution!® Book 051. (Just Think about the Multitude of almost Worthless Meetings of the Minds, who Strained themselves to Think of Reasonable Solutions for our Massive Problems, who sometimes even Prayed to God for Help; but, the Solutions have been here for no less than 40 Years — Thanks to the Spirit of Inspiration from GOD!)

[_] 40-52 — **"Are we Tax Slaves of a Lower Order than those Lying Edomites!"** (HOW to be Liberated from all Slavery, Worldwide!) By The Worldwide People's Revolution!® Book 052. {This Inspired Book once had another Title and Author, which was not Acceptable by Amazon, which has now been Restored in all of its Glory, and is Published by more Trustworthy People, who are not Afraid of Controversies, nor of: **"The Swanky Sword of Divine Truths!"** (The Most Powerful Weapon in the Whole Universe!) By The Worldwide People's Revolution!® Book 067.}

[_] 40-53 — **"The Great False Economy is now DEBUNKED!"** (Adolf Hitler had a much Better Economic System!) By The Worldwide People's Revolution!® Book 053. (Trust me,

Adolf was no Saint; but, during the Day of God's Judgment, he will be Justified, while his Anti-Christ Opponents will be Condemned: beCause they Refused to Attend a Worldwide Radio Debate with Adolf Hitler, whose Arguments will Stand Up during the Day of Judgment, which would have Prevented World War 2, and thus Saved the Lives of no less than 60 Million People! Likewise, we Tax Slaves must now Act more Wisely, and DEMAND **"The Great Worldwide TELEVISED Court HEARING,"** Book 041, whereby we might Save the World from that Dreadful Battle of Megiddo, called *Armageddon!* Yes, the Ball is now in YOUR Hands, my Potential Friend or Enemy, and you are now Responsible for it. Therefore, do not Shirk your Duty as a Free Citizen; but, Help us to Spread this Message far and wide, whereby the Masses of People will be Demanding The GWTCH, and thus Prevent another far more Dreadful and Hateful World WAR!)

[_] 40-54 — **"The UGLY Scarred Dishonest Face of Poor Old Miserable UNCLE SAM!"** (A Memorial Day Legacy!) By The Worldwide People's Revolution!® Book 054. {NOTE: This Inspired Book was also Suppressed by Amazon, who will be most Ashamed of themselves if they do not Un-suppress it during the Future: beCause it will also be Published by People of Greater Faith, who Know for a Fact that it is the TRUTH! Therefore, joust be Patient.}

[_] 40-55 — **"The United States of the Whole World!"** (A True Global Economy for the Masses of Working People!) By The Worldwide People's Revolution!® Book 055. (This Inspired Book contains many Colored Photographs with Explanations. It is a Good Book to Publish in Foreign Nations, who are not so Blinded by their Pride, who can See the Mountain of Lies much Better at a Distance from them: beCause of not being a Part of the American Corruption.) †‡

[_] 40-56 — **"The New RIGHTEOUS One-World Government!"** (HOW to Establish a Righteous One-World Government without Going to WAR!) By The Worldwide People's Revolution!® Book 056. (This is a KEY Book, which everyone should Study Carefully and Prayerfully.)

[_] 40-57 — **"Those Ridiculous Contradictions within the Holy Bible!"** (HOW to Read the Mutilated Bible with an Open Mind!) By The Worldwide People's Revolution!® Book 057. (Many Professing "Christians" Falsely Claim that their so-called *"Holy Bibles"* do not Contain any Contradictions, being "the Infallible Inspired Word of the Living God," but, without the Capitalized Words, and without Explaining just WHY there are more than 200 Contradictory Versions of it! This Book Reveals how to Deal with those Biblical Problems, and come to Understand WHY God Allowed it to Happen for the Truth's Sake. Trust me, you have never Heard this Explanation before now.)

[_] 40-58 — **"The Divided States of United Lies!"** (The so-called "United States of North America" in Disguise!) By The Worldwide People's Revolution!® Book 058. {NOTE: This is perhaps the most Referred to Book among all of the Books by our Selected King; but, that does not Mean that it is his Best Book by any Means, which is Well Camouflaged: so that it will Survive the Test of Time, even if the others are BURNED by the Anti-Christ Followers of Satan, who are Possession Worshipers of the Worst Kind, who Seek to Justify American Lies, rather than Quickly Confess them, and thus Escape from their Self-made Prison of Propagandish Lies! Just be Perfectly Honest, and you will have no Problem with any of our Literature.}

(HOW all People can Prosper in a RIIT WAA, and Stop Polluting the Earth with Capitalist TRASH!)

[_] 40-59 — "The Complete SURVEYS of our VALUES!" (SURVEYS of Religious Spiritual Political Governmental Sexual Social Moral Economic Business Labor Habitual and Miscellaneous VALUES!) By The Worldwide People's Revolution!® Book 059. {NOTE: According to our Selected King, every Potential Leader in the World must Fill Out and File those Surveys on the Internet for everyone to Study, whereby the Best People might be Elected by those Wise People who have also Filled Out the Complete Surveys of their own Values, whereby they will be Qualified to VOTE. Otherwise, they will not be Qualified to Vote, which will Eliminate a LOT of Wasted Money on Election Deceptions, while at the same Time it will Educate a lot of Ignorant People, who Desperately Need to Study that Inspired Book before Voting for another Dimwitcrat, Reprobate, or Independent Jackass!}

[_] 40-60 — "HOW to Get our PRIORITIES in ORDER!" (The Glories of Democracy; and, Does DEMON-ocracy have its Priorities in Order?) By The Worldwide People's Revolution!® Book 060. This Book will need to be Re-written by a Collective Group of Wise People, who will Contribute their True Life Stories during the Future, when they Wake Up and come to their Right Senses with the Prodigal Son of *Luke 15*. See:

[_] 40-61 — "The New MAGIFIED Version of The GOOD NEWS According to Saint LUKE!" (The Magnified Gospel of Saint Luke in Plain English!) Book 061, which is by Far the Best Version of that Gospel on the Earth, which has no Rivals at all among the other 200+ Versions. Guaranteed!

[_] 40-62 — "The New MAGNIFIED Version of The GOOD NEWS According to Saint JOHN!" (The Gospel According to Saint John Zebedee Boanerges in Plain English!) Book 062, which also has no Rivals among all of the other Versions: beCause this is no Translation of anything; but, it is the Inspired Words of the Living God, which were Revealed by the Holy Spirit, who has not Died.

[_] 40-63 — "The New MAGNIFIED Version of the Book of ACTS!" (The Understandable Version of the Acts of the Apostles in Plain English!) By The Worldwide People's Revolution!® Book 063. (This Inspired Book makes it Understandable WHY the Jews Hated the Apostles so much. You will have to Read it to Believe it.)

[_] 40-64 — "The New MAGNIFIED Version of the PSALMS of King David!" (The Understandable Version of the Famous Psalms in Plain English!) Book 064. You will be Amazed!

[_] 40-65 — "A List of FAIR Swanky Wages!" (The Equitable Wage System!) By The Worldwide People's Revolution!® Book 065. (All Hardworking People will LOVE this Good Book!)

[_] 40-66 — "Beautiful Swanky PALACES!" (A New Concept in Living Habits — Swanky Palaces for Poor People!) By The Worldwide People's Revolution!® Book 066. (You have no Idea what a "Swanky Palace" IS, unless you have read this Unique Book.)

[_] 40-67 — "The Swanky Sword of Divine Truths!" (The Most Powerful Weapon in the Whole Universe!) Book 067. (The very Reason that our Selected King has no Rivals is beCause of the Swanky Sword of Divine Truths, which no one can Defeat by any Means. Therefore, you Need to have it on your own Side, whereby no one can Defeat your Arguments! Be Strong, be Brave, have Faith and put on the Whole Armor of GOD!)

[_] 40-68 — "Has your Life become Extremely Complicated?" (HOW to Live a SIMPLE Life!) By The Worldwide People's Revolution!® Book 068. (Many People are not even Aware of just how Complicated their Lives are, until suddenly they are ready to Commit Suicide! It is Best to Prevent all such Evil Things, and this Book tells HOW.)

[_] 40-69 — "The IDEAL Place to Live!" (HOW to Discover the Ideal Place to Live!) Book 069.

[_] 40-70 — "Our Elected King Who Speaks Out!" (It is High Time for some Sane Person to Get Control of this Insane World!) By The Worldwide People's Revolution!® Book 070. (This Inspired Book contains a Special Speech that is Addressed to both Houses of the Congress in Washington. You will Love it, O Man of Greater Faith!)

[_] 40-71 — "How GAY is GOD?" (Oh the Wonders of it all when it ALL Hangs Out!) Book 071. (Do not Judge the Book, until you have Carefully "Red" all of it. You will be Surprised by the Truths!)

[_] 40-72 — "LIGHTNING STRIKES Versus Lightning Bugs and Impotent Fireflies!" (A Memorial Photo Album of some Real American Heroes!) By The Worldwide People's Revolution!® Book 072. (NOTE: This Book is Unique among all of the Books by our Selected King: beCause he did not get to Proof-read it before the Computer Crashed. It just Happened to be Saved on a Computer Chip before the Computer Crashed, and therefore it was Saved in PDF. But, the Corrections did not get made, which makes it a Special Collector's Item, which has more than 100 Colored Photos, which was what Caused the Crash.) †‡

[_] 40-73 — "The BEST of CAPITALISM!" (Corrections for: "LIGHTNING STRIKES Versus Lightning Bugs and Impotent Fireflies!") Book 073. (It is a completely new Book, except for those Corrections; and it is one of the Best Books in the World, which all Honest People will Love.)

[_] 40-74 — "LIGHTNING STRIKES Versus Lightning Bugs!" (HOW you can Become Moderately RICH, without Telling any Lies nor Selling any Trash!) By The Worldwide People's Revolution!® Book 074, which is the Perfection of all of the Lightning Striking Books, which is Recommended above all others for Mass Production: beCause it stands the Best Chance of being a Real Winner, just after this Book that you are now Reading, which has a Magnetizing Title!

[_] 40-75 — "What are the Punishments for Dietary Sins?" (Have we Served ourselves Well at the Tables of our Lusts?) Book 075. (This Book is too Controversial to be Published at this Time. Be very Patient until it is Available: beCause it is HOT!)

(HOW all People can Prosper in a RIIT WAA, and Stop Polluting the Earth with Capitalist TRASH!)

[_] 40-76 — "What is WRong with those CRAZY CHRISTIANS?" (A Self-Examination of the Heart of the Body of Good Government!) By The Worldwide People's Revolution!® Book 076.

[_] 40-77 — "The Gospel According to our Elected King!" (The Good News from the Most Modern Perspective!) Book 077. (This is perhaps the Best Book that you will Discover on Amazon, which contains the Famous Sermon that Jonah gave to the Ninevites, plus a very Special Sermon by Jesus Christ, himself!)

[_] 40-78 — "The Root Cause for almost all Evils!" (The Strange Things that People Say and Do to Get more Money!) Book 078. (This Book contains many Colored Photographs with Fascinating Explanations!)

[_] 40-79 — "Orgimmick Gardening at its Best!" (HOW to Grow Delicious Satisfying Foods without a 10-Million-Dollar Investment!) By The Worldwide People's Revolution!® Book 079. (This Book also contains many Colored Photographs with Wonderful Explanations!)

[_] 40-80 — "Guaranteed Solutions!" (HOW to Solve our Local and Global Problems in the Most Rational Manner Possible!) Book 080. (See the Description on Amazon: because they Offer a ONE-MILLION-DOLLAR REWARD to anyone who can Prove our Selected King's Solutions to be WRong or Unworkable! Can you Beat that? Do you have all such Guaranteed Solutions? Only our Selected King has those Solutions: beCause God Blest him with those Provable Solutions, which can be Proven in any Courtroom with Law and Order.)

[_] 40-81 — "Mexicans are more Intelligent than Americans!" (A Unique Challenge to all Americans and Mexicans!) By The Worldwide People's Revolution!® Book 081. {NOTE: The Remaining 275 Inspired Books by the Author of this Book may only be found in English, until we can get them Properly Translated into other Languages. Shame on you People who Killed him, who Broke his Heart with your Unbelief. May God have Mercy on your Poor Wretched Souls.} †‡

[_] 40-82 — "¡Los Mexicanos son más Inteligentes que los Estadounidenses!" (¡Un Desafío Único para todos los Estadounidenses y Mexicanos!) By The Worldwide People's Revolution!® Book 082. {NOTA: Aquí está el primer Libro en Español, que puede no ser Perfecto; pero, es Perfectamente lo Suficientemente Bueno para Iluminar las Mentes de quien lo Estudia.}

[_] 40-83 — "Was Billy Graham Greatly Deceived?" (Giving Honor to whom Honor is Due!) By The Worldwide People's Revolution!® Book 083. {NOTE: If you know a Grahamite, please Direct him or her to this Inspired Book, whereby he or she might be Converted to the Truths within it, and thus be Saved from Grahamite Perversions. Thank you.}

[_] 40-84 — "The New MAGNIFIED Version of the Book of DEUTERONOMY!" (The Understandable Version of Deuteronomy in Plain English!) Book 084. This is actually one of the Best Books within the entire Holy Bible, and also one of the Longest; but, do not allow that Fact to Deter you by any Means: beCause, "the Bigger Book is Normally a Better Book," which is True of a lot of Books, including all of the above Books: beCause it is the Nature of the Holy Spirit to get into Long-winded Sermons, you might say, which is WHY the Apostle Paul Preached until Midnight in the Book of Acts, until some Boy fell from a Window and Killed himself, whom the Apostle Paul Raised Up from the Dead and went on Preaching until the Dawn of the Day! {See: **"The New MAGNIFIED Version of the Book of ACTS"** for the Finest of Details, Book 063.}

[_] 40-85 — **"All of the Arguments are in Favor of our Selected King, who has Zero Challengers!" (Before you Attend another Election Deception, you should Carefully Study this Inspired Book with an Honest Open Mind!) By The Worldwide People's Revolution!®** Book 085.

[_] 40-90 — **"A New Jerusalem in the Great State of Flexible Texas!" (HOW to make Good Use of the Mississippi River!) By The Worldwide People's Revolution!** Book 090.

(HOW all People can Prosper in a RIIT WAA, and Stop Polluting the Earth with Capitalist TRASH!)

The Enticement,

Our Selected King, has come up with a Brand New Economic System, which is a Foolproof Plan for making almost everyone in the World Moderately RICH! Therefore, do not Deprive yourself of this Wonderful Inspiring Book, which also Contains Chapters 16 through 21 of *the Book of Revelation* — that is, it Contains the NEW MAGNIFIED Version (NMV) of it, which is quite Amazing, which alone is well Worth the HIGH COST of this very Sarcastic Book, which also Contains some other Fascinating Scriptures to Tantalize your Spiritual Taste Buds, which only our Selected King has Perfected for Serious Readers — such as the NMV of the Parable of the Prodigal Son in Luke 15.

www.ingramcontent.com/pod-product-compliance
Lightning Source LLC
Chambersburg PA
CBHW062333220526
45469CB00008B/2693